ALSO BY ILAN STAVANS

CHILDREN'S BOOK

Golemito (with Teresa Villegas)

ANTHOLOGIES

The Norton Anthology of Latino Literature * *Tropical Synagogues* * *The Oxford Book of Latin American Essays* * *The Schocken Book of Modern Sephardic Literature* * *Lengua Fresca* (with Harold Augenbraum) * *Wáchale!* * *The Scroll and the Cross* * *The Oxford Book of Jewish Stories* * *Mutual Impressions* * *Growing Up Latino* (with Harold Augenbraum) * *The FSG Book of Twentieth-Century Latin American Poetry*

GRAPHIC NOVELS

Latino USA (with Lalo Alcaraz) * *Mr. Spic Goes to Washington* (with Roberto Weil) * *Once @ 9:53* (with Marcelo Brodsky) * *El Iluminado* (with Steve Sheinkin) * *A Most Imperfect Union* (with Lalo Alcaraz)

TRANSLATIONS

Sentimental Songs, by Felipe Alfau * *The Plain in Flames*, by Juan Rulfo (with Harold Augenbraum) * *The Underdogs*, by Mariano Azuela (with Anna More)

EDITIONS

César Vallejo: *Spain, Take This Chalice from Me* * *The Poetry of Pablo Neruda* * *Encyclopedia Latina* (4 volumes) * Pablo Neruda: *I Explain a Few Things* * *The Collected Stories of Calvert Casey* * Isaac Bashevis Singer: *Collected Stories* (3 volumes) * Cesar Chavez: *An Organizer's Tale* * Rubén Darío: *Selected Writings* * Pablo Neruda: *All the Odes* * *Latin Music* (2 volumes)

GENERAL

The Essential Ilan Stavans

RECLAIMING TRAVEL

ILAN STAVANS *and* JOSHUA ELLISON

RECLAIMING

TRAVEL

DUKE UNIVERSITY PRESS *Durham and London* 2015

© 2015 DUKE UNIVERSITY PRESS

All rights reserved

Printed in the United States of America on acid-free paper ∞

DESIGNED BY NATALIE F. SMITH

Typeset in Chaparral Pro by Westchester Publishing Services

LIBRARY OF CONGRESS CATALOGING-IN-PUBLICATION DATA

Stavans, Ilan. *Reclaiming travel / Ilan Stavans and Joshua Ellison.*

pages cm   Includes bibliographical references and index.

ISBN 978-0-8223-5869-5 *(hardcover : alk. paper)*

ISBN 978-0-8223-7559-3 *(e-book)*

1. *Travel.* 2. *Voyages and travels.* 3. *Tourism.* 4. *Travel writing.*

I. *Ellison, Joshua, 1978–* II. *Title.*

G156.S73 2015 910—dc23 2014033896

COVER PHOTO

Martin Parr, Venice, from *Home and Abroad*, 1990.

© Martin Parr / Magnum Photos.

There is no foreign land;
it is the traveler only who is foreign.

ROBERT LOUIS STEVENSON,
THE SILVERADO SQUATTERS (1883)

CONTENTS

INTRODUCTION

Restlessness

The world is still deceived with ornament.

WILLIAM SHAKESPEARE, *THE MERCHANT OF VENICE* (1605)

We are creatures in motion, of motion. George Santayana, in *The Philosophy of Travel,* called it the "privilege of animals"; the capacity to wander in search of better prospects is the key to our intelligence and imagination, unlike the plants that are "fatally rooted to the ground." The human story is, above all, an itinerary of endless departures and returns, advances and retreats, incursions and displacements.

This book ponders two simple—seemingly simplistic—questions: why we travel and how we travel. And, along the way, it tackles a third one: Is there a difference between travel and tourism? The answers are extraordinarily complex. We travel, in part, because we are restless. The word "restlessness" can describe so many things, at so many registers of emotional intensity, from passing boredom to the deepest existential angst. The restlessness we speak of here is something like what Bruce Chatwin, one of the twentieth century's most exemplary travelers, in an unfinished manuscript, called "the nomadic alternative." The yearning to explore our surroundings and understand our context is natural to us. A nomad, says Chatwin, is not one without a home—a nomad has the ability to be at home anywhere.

What is the nomadic alternative, exactly? Chatwin speculates that civilization itself is an accident of history—a peculiar happenstance that developed under exceptional conditions, long ago, in Mesopotamia. Civilization, defined by human settlement, is just a resilient variation along our evolutionary course. But his point is not so much anthropological (Chatwin himself called it a "dubious theory") as a thought experiment: Is there another, less encumbered, way for humans to exist? What is the natural state of our species, sedentary or mobile?

Looking into our past, and at the world around us, it seems we are wired for both. Most lives are refutations of the nomadic. Giambattista Vico, a Renaissance philosopher, believed that civilization stands on three principles of history: religion, marriage, and burial. Think of a cemetery in the shadow of a church: we are accustomed to their proximity. To bury our dead is to plant roots in the ground. The sanctuary is where the living go for respite; the home is our society in miniature; the grave is where the dead rest. The theater of life and death: our attachment to home encompasses everything from memory to presence to immanence.

On the other hand, civilization has obviously not cured us of our nomadic itch. Our relative prosperity hasn't made us sedentary. Mass movement—the transfer, temporary or permanent, of multitudes—is as fundamental to modern life as the Internet or the global flow of goods and capital. Tourism is a badge of status for travelers and a path to prosperity for hosts. Poor regions in South America and South Asia have made great strides through their tourist economies, with international visitor numbers leaping in the first decades of the twenty-first century. Even sub-Saharan Africa, which includes some of the most forlorn places on the planet, has seen significant upturns in tourism. Many of our most intractable challenges are directly linked to our mobility: scarcity, urbanization, environmental depletion, and, of course, immigration. Some two hundred million people are now living outside their country of birth.

Civilization and nomadism, far from being at odds, are really the twin impulses that make us human. The desire to travel is intimately connected with our idea of home. Identity and place are mysteriously but palpably entangled. Home is where we forge our sense of self, but we delineate its edges and push its boundaries by seeking out new challenges and surroundings. The experiences we have as children, and the memories they implant, link us to a place—and to an image of ourselves. Venturing out into the world is frightening. A child starts the process with her first steps, and again later, when she begins to wander beyond her parents' reach. That journey is how we discover who we are, our role in the world, and our sense of purpose.

"Human beings need to learn to be each other's guests on this small planet," writes George Steiner in one of his pieces in the collection *No Passion Spent*. Hospitality is a survival skill, long cultivated in migratory cultures. Immanuel Kant believed that hospitality was the only universal human right. Freedom of movement and access is a cornerstone of the "perpetual peace" that Kant envisions, as is the absolute right to seek refuge in a foreign land.

We usually focus on the ethical imperative of hospitality, on the obligation to be a generous host. When we travel, we are *asking for* hospitality. In a speech he delivered in 2003 upon receiving the Börne Prize, Steiner explained:

> A human being does not have any roots. He or she must make a pilgrimage through the human condition. That means we are all guests of life. Being is our host. We are life's invitees. . . . Human beings are reciprocally guests and hosts—just as both are the guests of life.

In the act of being received as visitors—if we travel with that role firmly in mind—we are cultivating a necessary species of humility. This is not simply a matter of common courtesy and respect for local customs. If we are to be transformed by our experiences of travel, we have to be malleable, agile, adaptable. Our ability to become "guests" gives us access to the invaluable variety of influences and perspectives that the world offers. Travel is a search for meaning not only in our own lives, but also in the lives of others. Of course, it is also a privilege, for while some people travel in search of inner growth and meaning, others die crossing borderlands and endure conditions of violence as they move around the world.

This book meditates, modestly, on some of the abiding mysteries of travel and place and about travel as an excess, even an abuse. It also looks closely and critically at how we travel today. In the past, travel has connoted exile, spiritual or prophetic searching, exploration, conquest, commerce. Most travel today is a form of personal enrichment: it's edifying, entertaining, and sometimes leisurely. How did we arrive here? What role does it play in our intellectual and cultural evolution? What is missing from our contemporary understanding of travel?

Simply dividing the world into travelers and tourists isn't enough. We have all been tourists at some point or other. That is to say, we have all allowed ourselves to be passive consumers of experience. We have all been inconsiderate guests. We have all chosen, from time to time, an easier path in our travels, as in many other domains of life. These are just facts of being human, and we need not castigate ourselves for it, even as we aspire to better. Because the kind of travel we talk about in this book is aspirational. It is achievable, but never entirely. A traveler is something we are at our best.

This book is about choices we all make in how we perceive ourselves and how we relate to the world. Our goal is not to chastise or ridicule. No one should avoid traveling out of fear of being—or being perceived as—a tourist. It is always safer, in a way, to just stay home. The risk of giving offense is much lower. So is the hazard of looking foolish. But risk taking is exactly the point. We hope that this book is read as an invitation to take risks, to try things that don't seem entirely comfortable at first. Frankly, the dangers of a world in which we all just mind our own business, in which we all just keep to our own kind, seem far more frightening.

The pronoun "we" serves us well. These reflections are a product of a sustained, symmetrical conversation in which two "I"s have merged into one. Not to say that we are without disagreement or divergent points of view. We hope to turn dissent into a flux: to deliberate by enfolding numerous perspectives. In other words, we see the *unum* as a conduit for the *pluribus*. There is another intention behind the "we": to create a bridge with the reader, to establish a common ground, in linguistic terms, where we all meet together in our inquiries. The pronoun is a common ground, conveying an all-seeing, always-thinking plural "I" that belongs to everyone and no one.

This isn't a conceit. Of course, we are aware of the drawbacks of such an encompassing, omnipotent narrative voice. Yet people, insofar as they share a time, have many common goals. The "we" invoked is thus the sum of who we are, not its reduction. This kind of collaborative writing is unusual, and it has its costs and its benefits. As we discuss in chapter 2, writing about travel is almost always connected with personal experience, with memory, with autobiography. Writing about specific personal experiences—that is to say, writing anecdotally—is impossible when you are writing for yourself but also on behalf of someone else.

Since our personal experiences of travel belong to us alone, they did not find their way into this book. One reason our book draws so heavily on literature is because it represents a reservoir of shared experience. This is part of literature's basic nature: stories reflect an author's point of view, her experience of the world, but only succeed if they meet with some kind of authentic recognition in the reader. So while we have limited ourselves by omitting personal narrative, this kind of writing has pushed us to go past anecdotes, to try to find in our own experiences something that feels mutual and inclusive.

The origins of *Reclaiming Travel* are in a homonymous op-ed piece we published in the *New York Times* (July 7, 2012). It was prompted by disquiet: the dissonance we experienced regarding the question of travel, our own frequent question, and that of those around us. It seemed to us that traveling was a robot-like endeavor: get out, explore a place, and get back. The motions were defined by platitudes. The excitement was mechanical, even methodical. Everything was new, yet nothing was.

The piece generated a heated debate, online and on the airwaves. We weren't alone, it was clear: the uneasiness was general.

This book is an expansion of that debate. It includes what we learned from the conversation, the reaction we experienced to our own argument. We are aware that reclaiming travel isn't done in writing. It is done in action, by reimagining a behavior that is ancestral, by creating a community of travelers eager to reaffirm meaning. As we state in these pages, travel and tourism are different: one seeks enlightenment while the other is content with thrills.

Why turn "Reclaiming Travel" into *Reclaiming Travel*? Because there is great pleasure—and great responsibility—in thinking things through. That's what books are about: digging into a topic until you get into its heart.

We approach this book like a voyage: full of interrogations, expectations, and trepidations. Our itinerary is rough and open to improvisation. At some destinations we will linger and at others we will pause only momentarily, just long enough to admit an impression, and then we will be off again. There will be comfortable surroundings and unfamiliar ones, too.

Our belief is that we urgently need to reclaim a definition of restlessness—"stirring constantly, desirous of action"—that signals our curiosity toward the world, our eagerness to explore outside the safe confines of the familiar. Travel should be an art through which our restlessness finds expression. We need to bring back the idea of travel as a search.

We have a long way to go.

PART I

Why We Travel

1

THE MOTION
OF MYTH

In 1875, Sigmund Freud traveled to England for the first time. Already nineteen, he was having his first glimpse of the sea. After a visit with relatives in Manchester, he set out for the shore. Standing on that beach, breathing the air, the great explorer of the human psyche experienced a strange feeling he would later describe in a letter: "One feels oneself like a hero who has performed deeds of improbable greatness."

Freud wrestled with the power of mythos—stories that probe the past for enduring human meaning—throughout his career. Much later in life, in *New Introductory Lectures on Psychoanalysis*, he wrote, "The theory of the instincts is, so to say, our mythology. Instincts are mythical entities magnificent in their indefiniteness." Myths are the stories the psyche tells itself.

Freud wrote about Greek and biblical characters not in literary terms but as avatars of powerful psychological forces. We retell the wretched story of Oedipus because it is too horrific to admit that we are living out a version of the same tragedy. Myths speak to us on behalf of our repressed urges and fears. This is what makes mythology useful to psychoanalysis: as a roadmap to an inner archaeology. Psychoanalysis, Freud said, is like "excavating a buried city."

It is either ironic or apt, depending on how you look at it, that Freud was a notoriously phobic traveler. For someone with strong convictions about the hidden mechanics of the psyche, the external world could be deeply unsettling for him. On his first visit to the Acropolis, he was overcome by a sensation he called "derealization," that uneasy feeling when you find yourself staring at a site you have known only in your mind's eye, in books, or in dreams. He was preoccupied by contradictory impulses: wanderlust, what Nabokov in *Mary* called "nostalgia in reverse, the longing for yet another strange land," and *Reisemalheurs*, German for "the misfortunes of travel," the fear of the unknown, the chaos of the voyage, the anxiety of being far from home. Freud traveled throughout his life, as both a tourist and a refugee; both filled him with wonder and dread. He placed travel at the very center of his understanding of human motivation. The pleasure of travel, he said, arises from the earliest desire to escape the father and the family.

It isn't surprising that Freud's mythic mode was awakened by the sea. Water is symbolic. We come from water. Water is bigger and stronger than us, irrepressible, unpredictable. There is both mystery and promise in the limitless expanse we see from the shore. We live most of our lives within well-defined boundaries, observing strict protocols; the ocean, like a clear night sky, is one of those rare encounters with infinity. It forces us to consider the fact that there is something out there, waiting for us, something we can't see yet. Facing the ocean at Blackpool, the teenage Freud must have sensed, perhaps despite himself, that he was standing at the frontier between reality and allegory. He must have known that he was at one journey's end and the beginning of another.

Joseph Campbell famously said, "Myths are public dreams, dreams are private myths." That is the core sensation of myth, the feeling that we're in a dream, and travel is a way of revealing—and reveling in—the dreamlike in us and outside us. We spend so much of our lives sharpening the characteristics that make us distinct. Myth is evidence that our personal quest isn't as personal—that is, as individualistic—as we might like to believe.

Wherever myths come from, whatever their relationship to reality, they speak authentically about what it is to be human.

Travel is not only a physical act. It is also a way to connect with the mythical dimension in our psyche. Myths epitomize human nature. The desire to explore a new landscape is connected with our inner drive to test ourselves, to prove our mettle in extraordinary circumstances. The repertoire of behaviors we employ in travel is usually not so unlike the activity of daily life. Humans are not as complicated as we like to think. We eat, sleep, walk, read, write, and so forth, wherever we are. Travel does not change our basic skill set so much as it demands that we perform under slightly modified conditions, so that we have to rethink decisions that happen automatically in daily life. To travel is to consent to the prospect and potential of the unfamiliar.

Journeys are at the heart of mythology. In the Bible, Adam and Eve, the first couple, are pushed out of Eden. Abraham's people are called Ivri—those who cross. For the Children of Israel, the experience of dislocation is so central to their identity that they carry it in their name. Noah, Abraham, Joseph, Moses: all outsiders who only realize their destinies through interruption and relocation. The Epic of Gilgamesh, the *Iliad* and *Odyssey*, and the Icelandic sagas are narratives about the itinerant life that, further, link travel to cosmology and often to creation itself. In these foundational texts, travel is both transformative and generative.

Mythology is, itself, a traveling genre. In the early Mediterranean world, there was an indissoluble link between exploration, conquest, trade, and storytelling. The strong familial resemblances among mythic heroes and narratives are the result of encounters along the trade routes and frontiers of the ancient world. Gilgamesh precedes Odysseus in a journey to the end of the earth. Sinbad the Sailor, of the *Thousand and One Nights*, has his own sightless sailor-eater to contend with, just as Odysseus blinded the Cyclops.

Hermes, the Greek god of travel, is also the deity of commerce, literature, and thieves. He moves shrewdly between the realms of gods and mortals. He is both a trickster and, in Homer, "the bringer of good luck." (Today he is immortalized as a luxury travel goods brand favored by rappers and prosperous Muscovites.) Hermes likely has an ancestor in the Egyptian god Thoth. The two have common attributes and careers. Thoth was an intermediary and a mediator. He was a scribe, a progenitor of language and a custodian of knowledge. Both Hermes and Thoth have the special talents of the migratory. Like nomadic people, they both have above-average gifts of persuasion and adaptation. They have the agility of wanderers and outsiders. And they are both storytellers and translators. Hermes is, of course, also the god of deceit. In other words, they are themselves mythmakers—and myth is the currency of itinerancy.

In ancient mythology, travel is a crucible in which greatness and insight are intensified. Some characters set out heroically on their journeys; others are conscripted. Jesus and Buddha both lit out into the wilderness, looking for enlightenment in seclusion and nature. When Moses encounters the burning bush he is minding his own business, tending his own flock—his is a journey of election rather than volition. Like Moses, Odysseus is pressed into service. But it is the journey itself that is the transfiguring part, more so than the exceptional spirit of the personality. Generally speaking, in myths, amazing exploits produce exalted heroes, and not the other way around.

Even the gods must sometimes travel. According to Yoruba mythology, in the beginning there was only sky and water. Obàtálá was a curious orisha, not content to live idly in the clouds. The other orishas were perfectly happy to luxuriate by the baobab tree, all their needs satisfied. But Obàtálá had the restlessness of an explorer. He collected all the gold he could find and made a chain by which he lowered himself, descending toward the primordial water. As he reached the end of his tether, he poured out a bag of sand. The sand scattered and dry land spread out beneath him (with the help of a white hen he had brought along for exactly this purpose, handily). He hopped down, went about creating the terrestrial world, and climbed back up again. A traveler to his core, Obàtálá is a strong presence in the religions of the New World as well. In Cuban Santería, for example, Obàtálá has been syncretized with the Virgin Mary. Believers make sacrifices to him—including, sometimes, a white hen.

In Bahia, northern Brazil, Candomblé is an African-derived religion that elides Yoruba, Fon, Ewe, and Bantu and has incorporated elements of Catholicism over time. The orishas are again central to the cosmology; lesser deities that serve a unitary god. Orishas personify natural forces, embody archetypes for human interaction. They are also the matrix through which African memory is transmitted and made relevant to new surroundings. As people sold into slavery by ship, they have an especially poignant relationship to Iemanjá, the orisha of the sea. The great novelist from Bahia, Jorge Amado, in *Sea of Death*, wrote about the poor fishermen who worship Iemanjá:

> The men from dockside only have one path in life: the path of the sea. They follow it. It's their fate. The sea owns all of them. From the sea comes all joy and all sadness because the sea is a mystery that not even the oldest sailors understand. . . . Who has ever deciphered the mystery of the sea? From the sea comes music, love, death. And isn't it over the sea that the moon is the most beautiful? The sea is unstable.

Syncretic religions like Santería and Candomblé are themselves by-products of travel. Syncretism is an amalgamation of parts, a joining of various ingredients that result in a new whole. When African slaves were relocated to the New World, they accommodated themselves to new spiritual needs in Brazil or Cuba (not to mention Miami and the Bronx) or anyplace they settled on this side of the Atlantic. They adapted the oldest forms of belief to harrowing new environments.

The explosion of religious creativity and innovation throughout the black Atlantic—with influences that reverberate from cosmology to music—must be among the great feats of human ingenuity. At the intersection of colonial, slave, and indigenous peoples—a meeting of unequals but each part rich in belief and imagery—discrete traditions collided and elided. The spirits are not just analogues to the Catholic saints: they are traveling companions. Saints and spirits walk together.

THE *ODYSSEY* IS a homeward journey. *Nostos*, in Greek νόστος, means returning home. It is what impels Odysseus—he "kept turning his face at the blazing Sun, impatient for it to set, as he was longing to be on his way." His restlessness is oriented toward the familiar, toward reunification. Of course, Odysseus's voyage back to Ithaca is only half his journey. The quest begins in the *Iliad*. Together the two sagas make for a complete narrative, departure and arrival. And yet that second part is the most memorable, and not only because of its superior verse. Nostos is also a poetic genre of the classical world: the sea journeys of Greek heroes returning from Troy. Ovid, in his *Tristia*, sums it up in a line: "I must be forever deprived of my native land, unless the wrath of the injured god be softened."

Traveling isn't only a matter of leaving; it is about coming back, transformed. The motif of recognition is used in the Homeric tradition for great dramatic effect and narrative twists: Will Penelope recognize Odysseus? The nurse identifies Odysseus by his scar! Odysseus and Telemachos recognize each other as father and son! But, melodrama aside, this motif tells us something important about the nature of the journey and the homecoming. How has the experience changed us? In what sense are we different? Odysseus is altered by the challenges he faces, the encounters with deities, the foes he vanquishes.

We leave home in one way and come back in another. The person who departs and the one who returns aren't the same. A transformation occurs; or better, a metamorphosis. The person before and the person after might share the same features (name and address, demeanor and disposition), but their inner truths are different. There's no guarantee that the changes will be profound, easily perceived, or even, on the whole, positive. But in one way or another, the traveler is richer than before. In short, travel at its best gives us access to what we might have previously believed to be beyond our grasp. It enlarges the scope of our thinking, gives a larger context to our self-understanding.

Odysseus's journey home after the fall of Troy is a canvas on which we, its readers, are also depicted. Ithaca is not only a remote island in the country we still call Greece. It is also the place each of us calls home. That place exerts magnetic power on us. Whenever we leave it, our Ithaca calls us back. We all live some version of the tug-of-war between our Calypsos and Penelopes. The contemporary American poet Louise Glück, in her book *Meadowlands*, draws explicitly on this tradition, inverting nostos to tell the very modern story of a disintegrating marriage and a husband who is being pulled away from home:

Now the spell is ended.
Give him back his life,
sea that can only move forward.

In Glück's version, the protagonist is both Odysseus and Penelope. She is the one left behind, and also on her own journey toward a past that can't be retrieved. In a poem titled "Nostos," Glück implies that experience itself is only remembrance and longing for home: "We look at the world once, in childhood / The rest is memory."

Journeys are necessary for myth, because mythological thinking entertains the promise of better worlds, just over the horizon. The mythic voyage—like its devotional counterpart, the pilgrimage—depends on a cosmos with a *here* and a *there*. Here is profane; there is sacred. The word "paradise," for example, is a portmanteau of Hebrew, Greek, and Persian. Its roots suggest a walled garden, evoking Eden. So paradise is an enclosed and enthralling world, fundamentally separate from the one we inhabit. This helps explain the common travelers' preoccupation with authenticity—everyone wants to see the real Paris or the real India, which is to say, the real experience of a place that is unvarnished by our presence as outsiders. It also must be more real than the place we set out from. Paris has to be more cultured;

India has to be more spiritual and primitive. As Mircea Eliade writes, "The 'real' must always be elsewhere, an orderly 'paradise' that contrasts with the chaos of the present environment."

Thomas More constructed his Utopia exactly this way: a remote and unspoiled island. The name Utopia, in Greek, puns on the phrases "good place" and "no place." More understood that the power of his creation was its impossibility. It mattered because it wouldn't—it couldn't—ever really exist. Francisco de Quevedo, the extraordinary Spanish baroque poet, ridiculed the idea of the New World as a utopia, stressing that human foibles were as likely to occur in the lands "discovered" by Columbus as in the faraway places of Marco Polo.

There are plenty of details in More's world that have proven to be prescient, or at least comprehensible to a modern reader. There are attractive points, like universal health care and religious tolerance. More also has what we might call an overdeveloped sense of justice: premarital sex is punished by enforced celibacy (lifetime); criminals become slaves; women must confess their sins to their husbands. Some of these features square neatly with More's patrician Catholicism, but his Utopia is not a fundamentalist haven. In many ways, this imagined society was more liberal than what More himself would likely endorse.

Though More writes, "There are many things in the commonwealth of Utopia that I rather wish, than hope, to see followed in our governments," he is emphatically not building a habitat to his own specifications, and it is certainly not meant to replicate any society More had ever experienced. This is an idealized world, to be sure, but it's not the Kingdom of Heaven. That ambiguity is what makes the work more interesting than a mere political allegory. There are too many contradictions, too many compromises, to imagine that More might have felt unambiguously at home in his own Utopia.

In the New Testament's Epistle to the Hebrews, the narrator offers up comfort to the persecuted: "For there we have no lasting city, but we seek the city that is to come." Not all homecomings are returns, at least not in a literal or geographic sense. Home-

coming is a perennial metaphor for death, redemption, and res-
toration. Augustine of Hippo wrote his book *City of God* shortly
after the sack of Rome by the Visigoths. Augustine's vision of a
heavenly city, like the Epistle to the Hebrews, was written as a
balm for the followers of the Church, which was still young. Don't
get too attached to the city of this world, he argued, because a
Christian's true home is in heaven. The book of Romans warns,
"Do not be conformed to this world." On the mortal plane, the
Christian is a foreigner and an outsider. The apostle Peter puts it
thus: "Dear friends, I urge you, as foreigners and exiles, to abstain
from sinful desires, which wage war against your soul."

In short, the true Christian is just a tourist here, enjoying the
sights, but also impatient to get home. He can exist in the earthly
world and still remain aloof, Augustine believes: "For as long as
the two cities are commingled, we also enjoy the peace of Babylon. For from Babylon the people of God is so freed that it mean-
while sojourns in its company." In the world, but not of it.

Nostos is alluring, sometimes sublime, but also hazardous. It
can leave the afflicted despairing and disconnected. It's the active
element that creates nostalgia, which can distort our recollection
and amplify our alienation. In seeking to return home, we blind
ourselves to the beauties of the journey: it is the past, not the
present, that matters. In his poem "The Return of the Exile," the
modern Greek poet George Seferis—evoking the *Odyssey*—has
a cautionary message for a refugee returning home after many
years away.

> My old friend, stop a moment and think:
> you'll get used to it little by little.
> Your nostalgia has created
> a non-existent country, with laws
> alien to earth and man.

T. S. Eliot proposed that mythology should be the basis for literature going forward, supplanting narrative and even character.
Mythos, he wrote in his essay "*Ulysses*, Order and Myth," offered
"a way of controlling, of ordering, of giving shape and significance

to the immense panorama of futility and anarchy which is contemporary history." Through myth we persuade ourselves about wholeness.

James Joyce took the *Odyssey* as the gateway into his masterwork. In *Ulysses*, the protagonist, Leopold Bloom, wanders unheroically through Dublin. The *Odyssey*'s ten-year journey is compressed into a single day. The banality of his adventures, contrasted with Odysseus's heroism, feels like a sour rebuke of the mythic ideal. In his barbaric age, Joyce had little use for the fabulism of Homer. This was not a test from the gods; humankind was very much on its own. Joyce took exile to be decisive for his identity and obligatory for his art.

EXILE IS THE mythic journey's melancholy counterpart. It is the myth without the redemption. Genesis alone tells of three exiles: the eviction from Eden, the banishment of Cain, and the scattering of the builders of Babel.

In Exodus, God reminds the wandering Israelites that he delivered them from Egypt on "eagles' wings." The former slaves are three months into their wandering, the text tells us, which we know to mean that they still have a long way to go. Even a casual acquaintance with the Exodus story should make that phrase seem strange. With all the tribulations they had faced, and the countless more to come, does it sound right to say that the Israelites were lifted like a bird, that they soared to freedom? The metaphor just seems wrong. They didn't coast above the Red Sea, after all. They trudged through the mud.

Most commentators take the phrase as an image of paternal care. If that's so, it's significant, then, that this biblical notion of divine love doesn't preclude the suffering the Israelites faced. We presume that God could have spared them the trouble. But he didn't. Why not?

This wandering and suffering are clearly integral to the narrative purposes of the Bible. Exile functions as a kind of spiritual purification that prepared the Israelites for emancipation. But to fully appreciate the significance of the exile, we can't be timid when confronting the human costs. No one who left slavery in Egypt made it to the Promised Land. Not even Moses. This was not a trial of faith. It was a purge. A bloodletting.

Exile arguably became Judaism's central motif during the Second Temple period, which turned out to be an interim between major dispersals. Exile became more than a territorial condition. It became an encompassing metaphor, not bounded by temporal or geographic specificity. It took on psychological, literary, and metaphysical dimensions. Even though the Temple had been restored and the nation had been repatriated, exile hung over Israel like a lingering scent. The prophet Ezra wrote ominously:

> But now, for a brief moment, the LORD our God has been gracious in leaving us a remnant and giving us a firm place in his sanctuary, and so our God gives light to our eyes and a little relief in our bondage.

"A brief moment" is about as succinct a statement of Jewish skepticism as we could want; in fact, this is where the tradition veers close to nihilism. But the moral dilemma of exile and suffering is very real and pressing: If God is all-powerful, he can't possibly be good, and if God is good, he certainly can't be all-powerful.

The prophet Ezekiel was among those deported from Jerusalem to Babylon in 597 BCE. He has a vision of the city in ruins. He watches the presence of God rise up and leave the city behind, following the exiles to the east. In other words, God moves. He is the god of the people, not of a particular place, and he goes with them into exile. Many years later, Jewish mysticism (Kabbalah), forged by the dizzying trauma of the Iberian expulsion, put exile at the center of its cosmological understanding of the universe. God's consummate act was contraction, rather than enlargement. In other words, it was a self-exile.

But the Kabbalists did not invest exile with valor because it was a condition shared with God. On the contrary, Gershom Scholem, the influential scholar of Jewish mysticism, in his definitive work on Kabbalah, called *Major Trends in Jewish Mysticism*, writes, "Absolute homelessness was the sinister symbol of absolute godlessness." Like the metaphor of the eagles' wings, this mystical worldview betrayed a truth that we usually prefer not to admit, and that religious interpreters have worked hard to explain away: if God is responsible for our expulsion, then it is an act of vengeance, not love.

The philosopher Baruch Spinoza, a radical Jewish thinker who in the seventeenth century was excommunicated from his community in Amsterdam, might be the first exile in the modern sense. His dislocation was individual, not communal. His insights into metaphysics were profoundly shaped by his acute isolation. Spinoza asserted, "God is immanent, not transcendent." Contrary to popular belief, Spinoza was not for pantheism or nature worship per se. There is a much more subtle idea at play here, and it is laced with the irony of the author's seclusion. Spinoza's God is something of a loner, too. In other words, a man who understood far better than most what it meant to be nowhere had a unique capacity to imagine a God that was everywhere, depersonalized, with infinite attributes and no exclusive domain—that is to say, no home.

The first modern exile, the first to live apart from a religious community, was also uniquely able to implode the barriers between *here* and *there* (contra Augustine), and between the internal and external world. After Spinoza—and also because of Spinoza—our metaphoric relationship to exile has been desacralized, but it is still potent.

The Palestinian writer and thinker Edward Said is perhaps the most sensitive student of exile in the contemporary, secular sense. In his essay "Reflections on Exile" he describes both the nobility and the humiliations of life for the displaced, homeless, and outcast. His strength is to understand the full scope of the exilic experience, in both its symbolic force and its human deprivations. (The essay begins, "Exile is strangely compelling to think about but terrible to experience.") He balances the intellectual deftness that exile can afford with the abject brokenness that it can leave behind. Said makes the supremely moral argument that "exile is neither aesthetically or humanistically comprehensible" and he is critical of the literature that valorizes it and "banalizes its mutilations."

The meaning of exile was transformed in the twentieth century in two key ways, one anthropological and one theoretical. Territorial displacement became a mass phenomenon, affecting millions and exerting a profound influence on geopolitics. In that same century, we might also say that exile replaced the heroic journey as the vital mythic mode. Exile has been both generalized and internalized: modern life is fractured, disorienting, craving certainties that can't be delivered. Exile today is the realization that we will never be totally satisfied. (Said observes, "The intellectual in exile tends to be happy with the idea of unhappiness.")

"The exile therefore exists in a median state," he writes, between worlds and belonging nowhere in particular, or nowhere entirely. In the Augustinian sense, in it but not of it. For exile, intrinsically, is about loss of self and, in equal measure, about loss of words—or, better, about loss of worlds. In exile we are constantly reinventing ourselves in order to survive. We think we know who we are but we don't—we are incapable of it. To live in exile is to realize that confusion is the sine qua non of existence: to know is not to know and vice versa. This is what German critic Theodor Adorno means when he suggests in *Minima Moralia* that one has a moral imperative "not to feel at home in one's own home."

What's lost in exile—a sense of completeness, our faith that we each have a coherent self with a point of view—also gives the exiled some distinct advantages. There is a felicity of mind that comes with a strong sense of life's basic contingency; these are the qualities that engender irony, audacity, and improvisation. Albert Camus, in *The Rebel: An Essay on Man in Revolt*, wrote, "We all carry within us our places of exile, our crimes, and our ravages."

Perhaps exile is the reality that myth, and maybe even travel, exists to soothe: an insufficient response to our essential brokenness. The towering Bengali intellectual Rabindranath Tagore understood this distinction perfectly. Tagore himself led a peripatetic life. He was a cosmopolitan, in that he abhorred nationalism and parochialism, and he was also a nomad. He was both an aficionado and a skeptic when it came to myth. But his sense of exile was finely honed. In a poem titled "A Woman on a Pilgrimage," he writes:

> And at the end of her days
> the frustrated hopes of a neglected life
> are out to find a home
> in some distant land unknown.
> The day she started on her journey
> the sky smiled at her
> in fresh sunlight.
> Today, where she finds herself,
> the strangers around and their unfamiliar voice
> appear as so much meaningless noise.

2

INWARD VOYAGE

Travel and memory walk hand in hand. We couldn't travel without memory. It's what allows us to find our way home. Just as we feel a sense of place most acutely while we are in transit—going somewhere, leaving somewhere—we comprehend time by watching it recede. We experience time as memory: it flows ahead and disappears at the same time.

Our movements through space are registered by our topographic memory and then encoded as storytelling. Still, reminiscing about travel is mined with tricks. The story contaminates the experience from the very beginning, before we ever leave home. In some way, we never leave home when we travel. It is a voyage in our own mind. Even before we set out, we are already telling the story. We are already thinking of the potential audience, what they expect from us, and what we expect from them, as well. We reformulate and embellish. The story of the journey is never the journey itself: it is at best a summation, based on past events but delivered for the listeners in front of us at the moment of retelling. And each time it is repeated, the voyage changes. Are we untruthful? Not necessarily. Between the past and the memory of the past there is always a gap. That gap is called perspective.

To reminisce is to let the recounting replace the counting. In his autobiography, *My Last Sigh*, Spanish avant-garde filmmaker Luis Buñuel writes, "Our memory is our coherence, our reason, our feeling, even our action." He concludes, "Without it, we are nothing." Through memory, we build a personal narrative that defines our existence. We accumulate the necessary details from which a complete portrait emerges.

That narrative is fragile. It is also a form of self-delusion. For there is no way to prove that the past as we remember it is actually the past as it was lived. In other words, the past is always subjective, biased. The past is personal. In *The Man with a Shattered World: The History of a Brain Wound*, Russian neurologist A. R. Luria describes the fate of a soldier wounded during World War I. The wound cut him off from his mnemonic reservoir. He spent years resurveying that reservoir in order to know who he was, where he came from, or his expectations from life. In other words, the patient treated by Luria ceased to be himself because he couldn't remember anything about his past. He was no longer himself because there was no narrative to describe his existence. In some way, we are all people with a shattered world. We don't need to suffer a brain injury to censor particular elements. Of course, Luria's patient was an extreme case. But we are cases all the same: less dramatic but not less inventive.

Likewise with travel: what we experienced is only what we remember. We massage the past, package it, individualize it. Humans in general have a poor recall for facts and details. In that regard, our brains are highly imperfect machines and not always, it would seem, on our side. On the other hand, we are very adept at remembering acquired skills (as the saying goes, like learning to ride a bike), conjuring atmosphere and feelings, and creating meaning from our memories.

From a trip we took, we may retain a handful of mnemonic snapshots. Then we build a narrative around those snapshots. That, in the end, is what the trips are about: not what happened, but the story we tell ourselves about what happened. All journeys are recounted from that never-ending present. We can recall our first trip to a place, say Morocco, but we'll never actually be able to remember what it felt like to experience Morocco as a person who had never been there before. As soon as we arrived, that person was gone.

Linguists have argued that only speakers of languages with verbal tenses can comprehend a distinct past, present, and future. Without the "I was," "I am," and "I will be," we exist on a floating coordinate of space but not of time. To experience time, our language must be able to describe its gradations. Attention is given retrospective shape through memory. Its structure, its cadence, and its rhythms are analyzed.

Knowledge is not information; it is information turned into insight. Knowledge is memory transformed into value. Information is always impersonal whereas knowledge, like memory, isn't. Anyone might produce information. Knowledge, on the other hand, results from particular circumstances. We can learn about another person's history but we can't experience her memories. Memory is the main vehicle by which we experience consciousness. We are what we remember.

Memory fills in the gaps of travel, but travel also fills in gaps in our memory: missing episodes, unrealized opportunities, interrupted joy. Michel de Certeau, the French Jesuit whose work brought Jacques Lacan together with Saint Ignatius, wrote in *The Practice of Everyday Life*:

> What does travel ultimately produce if it is not, by a sort of reversal, "an exploration of the deserted places of my memory." . . . What this walking exile produces is precisely the body of legends that is currently lacking in one's own vicinity; it is a fiction, which moreover has the double characteristic like dreams or pedestrian rhetoric, or being the effect of displacements and condensations.

There is no memory without imagination, and vice versa. What we don't know, we invent. That invention is our contribution to the past. Imagination comes in to alleviate the disasters of forgetting: what we don't recall of the trip, we fantasize—we curate.

Often we are scavenging for fragments of identity and innocence that we shed along the routine passage of life and time.

LITERATURE NEEDS JOURNEYS because life doesn't come with inherently meaningful beginning and end points. We don't decide when we are born and most people don't have a say in when they die. And, before life and after death, we are rarely in a position to write about it. The very fact that travels have beginnings and endings is what gives them significance. Journeys give structure, because structure defines them; there is really no such thing as an eternal journey. Perpetual motion is possible in theory but not in nature. Doesn't narrative by definition imply movement and change, and doesn't that by definition epitomize travel?

V. S. Naipaul, in whose oeuvre literature and travel meet, has spent immeasurable time on the road. The record of that time is conveyed in astonishing narratives (*An Area of Darkness*, *The Loss of El Dorado*, *Among the Believers*, *A Turn in the South*), all of which are delivered in the past tense. A generous number of his books are detailed chronicles of journeys across Asia, Africa, Latin America, and the United States. He is the protagonist in them; his voice unifies those narratives. What he sees, what he hears, what he eats is recounted to the reader. Naipaul's travels are, as much as they are about his external experiences, about the inner dialogue he sustains with himself. That inner dialogue manifests itself through his methodical writing. Everywhere he goes he takes a notebook, which catalogs his adventures. He writes down his impressions: the way a landscape looks, the face of a little girl, a conversation with a waiter. He explains in an interview with the *Paris Review*:

> The trouble is that I can't go places without writing about them. I feel I've missed the experience. I once went to Brazil for ten days and didn't write anything. Well, I wrote something about Argentina and the Falklands, but I didn't possess the experience—I didn't work at it. It just flowed through me. It was a waste of my life. I'm not a holiday taker.

The notebook records Naipaul's movements and encounters; it does not yet tell a story. Not until Naipaul returns home does he actually devote himself to constructing the narrative of his voyage. He looks at the material *sub specie aeternitatis*: as a whole and from afar. He finds common themes that might not have been accessible during his note-taking efforts. He connects anecdotes that might have seemed disconnected at the time. He turns the parts into a whole.

Travel writing doesn't typically happen on the road, or at least not exclusively. Travel writing is not journaling. The e-mails we send home from exotic Internet cafés, or the daily status updates on Facebook, are not travel writing—not yet, anyway. The creditable part of the writing only happens when the author has had the time to properly grapple with the experience, as she remembers it. One must arrive at a place of being before one can tell a story about becoming.

Still, most people recognize that there is something called travel writing or a person called a travel writer. Travel writing has been happening in some form or other since antiquity. Sometime around the fifth century BCE, Hanno the Carthagian (also called Hanno the Navigator) wrote an episodic account of his naval explorations of the West African coast. He traveled at least as far as Morocco, and possibly as far as Cameroon, founding a half-dozen or so cities along the way. He claimed to travel with sixty ships and thirty thousand sailors, though it's not clear how he got five thousand people on each ship.

Written in Phoenician but surviving in Greek translation, his account is believed to be the oldest known example of travel writing in the West. The text—belonging to a genre known as *periplus* or "sailing around"—is an ordered, descriptive account of various ports and landmarks, including peoples encountered and noteworthy sights. The genre was mostly technical, though later examples blend with literary formulas.

The history of travel writing is essentially a transition from chronicle to anthropology to autobiography. Travel started as subject and has evolved into a device for self-exposition. Paul Fussell, the seminal critic of modern travel writing, in his book *Abroad: British Literary Traveling Between the Wars*, is characteristically clear on its definition: "a record of inquiry and the report of the effect of an inquiry on the mind and imagination of the traveler."

How we define travel writing tells us a lot about our attitudes toward travel. What we now call travel writing was usually branded, prior to the twentieth century, as "voyages and travels." It wasn't a genre in our modern sense, but simply a thematic flag. It was used to describe anything from a ship's log to slave narratives. There were few inherent claims about quality, veracity, or structure. The label, as it were, might apply to Samuel Johnson's *Journey to the Western Islands of Scotland*—but it could also include *Gilligan's Island*.

Defining the genre is not as easy as it might sound. By most common definitions, we are talking about a class of nonfiction. But it's not enough for the book to be about something that actually happened. And it's not enough to be about an actual place. After all, there are plenty of books that tell true stories set in actual foreign places. There are books that tell you true things about real places that also have no special interest in stories. If you pick up a Fodor's guide and read about a nearby museum, get a brief survey of its most impressive artifacts, and learn that it is closed on Mondays—you've read at least a kind of story about a real place that is presumably even true.

Fussell goes further in defining the modern travel book: it is an autobiographical account that "arises from the speaker's encounter with distant or unfamiliar data." He makes the bold assertion that, prior to 1750, "travel" didn't exist. Fussell argues that in the ancient world, though it had "plenty of movement from place to place," there was no travel in the sense we would recognize. Fussell has a strong sense of travel as a self-justifying end—in fact, self-justification is the only end that interests him. There is a teleological purity to his interpretation of history: "Before tourism there was travel, and before travel there was exploration." Each is roughly correspondent to an epoch of history, from the Renaissance to the industrial age to the age of mass leisure. This explains why his definition of travel writing is relatively narrow. Far from eternal, travel arose in a specific set of historical circumstances. Then, it ended.

At an opposite extreme, the writer Nicholas Delbanco, in a polemic book review in *Harper's Magazine*, suggests that all writing is travel writing: recording and reporting on unfamiliar places and sites and, ultimately, describing the changes that occur both internally and externally. Like the story of Abraham—the *lekh-lekha* episode in which God promises the future patriarch that, if he leaves his home in Mesopotamia for the promised land in Canaan, he will become the father of a great nation—all writing is about movement. Delbanco writes:

> In the Western tradition of literature, the common denominator of the *Odyssey* and *Pilgrim's Progress*, *The Canterbury Tales* and *The Divine Comedy*—not to mention *Don Quixote* or *Moby-Dick* or *Faust*—is near-constant motion.

Travel writing is related to memoir; the life story is circumscribed by a journey. The location is the frame, and the author is the canvas. Even if the story begins in medias res, there is an understood beginning—a departure—and a necessary resolution—a return. The itinerary is the organizing event, and it must include a return ticket. Or, if not a return, a new destination, a break in the action.

Travel writing is a form of thinking aloud, with the journey as the narrative frame. This elision of travel and thought—of travel as a metaphor for thoughts—has a long history. Our English word "theory" comes from the Greek *theorin*, which refers specifically to a journey beyond the city to witness an unfamiliar religious rite. As the anthropologist James Clifford, in "Notes on Travel and Theory," puts it so eloquently: "Theory is a product of displacement, comprising a certain distance. To theorize, one leaves home." Our ideas about the world are, or certainly should be, in close dialogue with our observations. This is a foundational notion for Western culture, but is not exclusive to the West. In

Hindi, the word *darshan* can refer to sight (vision, looking) and to insight (as in philosophy, a revelation, or heightened consciousness). For Hindus, it describes the encounter between human and divinity, meeting on the mortal plane, in the form of an avatar. Travel writing is, in large part, about self-interrogation as it emerges in a distant landscape.

Fussell suggests that the explosion of Anglo-American travel writing in the 1920s and 1930s—a high point, to his mind—was a response to the demise of the personal essay as a commercial genre. For writers like Aldous Huxley and Rebecca West, the travel book became a Trojan horse for "learned essays, which without exotic narrative support would find no audience." He describes West's magisterial and sprawling travelogue, *Black Lamb and Grey Falcon*, as a series of "ethical and historical essays" that are only secondarily the record of a journey through Yugoslavia. Jan Morris, known to most as a travel writer, agrees:

> I think of myself more as a belletrist, an old-fashioned word. Essayist would do; people understand that more or less. But the thing is, my subject has been mostly concerned with place. It needn't be.

Contemporary innovators in travel writing, such as Geoff Dyer, Rebecca Solnit, or John McPhee, have brought even more disciplines, or modes of literary expression, into the genre. While any of these writers is capable of delivering a gripping and vivid road narrative, they use that most familiar structure to scaffold dense hybrids that might include memoir, literary criticism, journalism, history, environmental activism, and science.

The confluence of travel writing and memoir is perfectly exemplified in the chronicles of immigrants. In the United States, Fanny Kemble, John James Audubon, Jacob Riis, Andrew Carnegie, and Mary Antin describe a kind of journey that isn't measured by miles but by emotional voltage. Their autobiographies are written in a second tongue, a language they were not born into. Their target reader is in the country that has welcomed them, that has given them a home. In fact, one of the most eloquent hymns to

travel is Emma Lazarus's sonnet "The New Colossus," engraved in
a plaque on the pedestal of the Statue of Liberty, one of the most
famous poems in the English language:

> Mother of Exiles. From her beacon-hand
> Glows world-wide welcome; her mild eyes command
> The air-bridged harbor that twin cities frame.
> "Keep, ancient lands, your storied pomp!" cries she

Lazarus's sonnet is an invitation to escape, to seek shelter, to be
received in a new land ready to take in those searching for a new
life. What makes "The New Colossus" enduring is its compassion:
no traveler will be turned back, no matter the background. In fact,
the Mother of Exiles favors the tired, the poor, the huddled masses.
The choice, if one is to be made, is on behalf of those who yearn to
breathe free. Lazarus wants the dreamers. Come to me, says the
mighty woman. I will light the road for you! You are the pilgrims
I'm looking for. You are the travelers that shall make this country
special.

Travel and immigration are not exactly the same, though immigration is a species of travel. All immigrants are looking for a fresh
start; all immigrants are ready to give up their possessions, the
narrative that defines them, in order to find a better place: a new
present tense. "The New Colossus" is this motherly figure—the
Statue of Liberty, a successor to the Colossus of Rhodes—but
might it not be as well the immigrant himself, sturdy, formidable
in his courage, venturing into unknown territory?

Immigrants travel lightly in terms of belongings but not in regard to memory. Aleksandr Solzhenitsyn, the Nobel Prize–winning
Russian author who spent years in Siberian exile before emigrat-
ing and settling in New Hampshire, wrote in his classic memoir,
The Gulag Archipelago:

> Own only what you can always carry with you: know languages,
> know countries, know people. Let your memory be your travel
> bag. Use your memory! Use your memory! It is those bitter
> seeds alone which might sprout and grow someday.

For immigrants, exile can be the only anchor. They find a new job, build a new home, learn a new language. But they keep their memories close at hand in order to articulate their new self, through the prism of the past. Their journey might take a day, a week, a month, although it is really life-long. A traveler has a place to return to, unlike the immigrant, who must start the long process of adapting her self-understanding to that new world.

Much travel is driven by the desire to set foot in unknown places, but there is also the travel of return, the journey to rewind the clock, to understand how the tree grew from the seed. Jamaica Kincaid returns to her native Antigua after years of life in the United States; Gabriel García Márquez, in *News of Kidnapping*, turns his attention to his native Colombia after years of exile.

The travel writing of the prodigal child, the return to a once-forsaken homeland, is an important contemporary variant. In some ways, these are journeys against time. By going back in time, we become someone other than who we are, who is still not who we were, either. The result is often painful, rarely completely satisfying. In the novel *Every Day Is for the Thief*, Teju Cole tells a quasi-fictional story of returning to Lagos, Nigeria, after many years in America. The scenes surrounding his arrival are the book's most affecting. The tension between those-who-left and those-who-stayed, such a fraught and common dynamic experienced by emigrants, is played out wonderfully at the airport. Jealousy and mistrust are palpable on both sides. Everyone is keenly aware how they appear to others, and how others reflect upon them.

> One man argues with a listless customs official about the inefficiency.

> —This is an international airport. It should be better run. Is this the impression visitors should have of our nation?

> The official shrugs, and says people like him should return home and make it better.

Soon after he arrives, the nameless protagonist describes walking into a family home that he hasn't seen since youth:

The house, of course, is unchanged. It is smaller only in memory. Memory and the intervening years, many of which I have spent in cramped English flats and American apartments, limitations I have endured like a prince in exile. Now, in the cool interior of this great house in Africa, proper size is restored.

It might be said that all voyages occur in Plato's cave. What we see along the way are shadows. Those shadows are our own projections, items we are looking for, emotions we seek to experience. The cave, of course, is our mind. But being trapped in one's mind is a form of hell. We long for experience because the mind is always at work and we look for recess, the opportunity to go outside ourselves. Yet, as we come back, as the memory of the trip comes together, we realize that even that was a kind of fiction. An invented story about ourselves and about the place we visited.

THERE IS A STORY about Gustav Mahler—two stories in fact, or a story told two ways with different meanings, and the difference hinges on a small but meaningful nuance of language. Around the time he was completing his Second and working on his Third symphonies, Mahler was spending his summers in a small mountain cottage by a lake near Salzburg. He built himself a little hut by the shore, just for composing. Mahler treated his hikes as ritual. He considered them indispensable to his work. William Wordsworth, in *Lyrical Ballads*, defined poetry as "the spontaneous overflow of powerful emotions recollected in tranquility." This is a good description of how Mahler used his time away from home and away from Vienna. It was solitary time. It was decompression, but also time to make productive sense of his discontents and exhilarations.

In 1896, his friend Bruno Walter, a rising conductor, visited him in the country. As the story goes, they were standing together by the hut, looking out at the mountains and the lake. They stood for a while silently, and then Mahler said something peculiar to Walter. This is where accounts diverge. There are several versions, but they come down to one or the other of the following:

1. "No use looking at that, I have composed all this already."
2. "No need to stare at those, I have already composed that all away."

The difference is slight, but it tells us a lot. Mahler had either composed it all or composed it all away. He had either translated the scene into music or, through his creative labor, freed himself from it.

In the first version, his music is an extension of his memory, a way to fasten down what he saw and felt. He was reporting back that he had completed the work of recording the scene. Maybe he is telling Walter: Don't worry about remembering this scene; I've got it all down.

What could the second version mean? It's much harder to say. Mahler was obsessed with the ungainly space where words, sounds, and images meet. He was mostly distrustful of words, but he had recognized limitations to all forms of perception and representation. Mahler often thought about his music in terms of images, and the Third is probably his most imagistic work. He gave the movements strange titles like "What the Flowers in the Meadow Tell Me" and "What Love Tells Me." He's offering each movement up as an explication of a scene or an experience, a sense impression, which speaks on behalf of the other senses. If we think Mahler told Walter that he had composed that all away, we get the bleak impression of a man to whom everything around him is speaking constantly; everything is alive and gasping. Everything reminds him of something else; nothing will let him forget. All he can do is try to keep up. Suddenly, the idyll of the mountains seems oppressive.

Or it may be something else entirely. Maybe his experiences in nature were a reservoir of inspiration that was spent in the act of writing music. By composing it away, he meant that it now belonged to the work only.

In both cases—and both versions—memory is at work, but in one it works on his behalf and in the other it seems to work against him. It seems possible that Mahler was both enriched and hounded by memory, and it's clear that place has an important role. Through his journeys into nature and through the act of composing, Mahler may have been walking both toward and away from memory. This was certainly true of the later Mahler, thinking about death as he wrote his Ninth, still working in the woods. In that symphony, in which death is also a journey, every stab at transcendence is scuttled by a childhood memory, like a melody or an image, which floats back in.

The Third ends with a famous theme that develops slowly and evocatively through the last movement. Years later, in 1938, on a different continent, the melody was lifted for a popular American song. Sammy Fain and Irving Kahal wrote a show tune that would be a postwar hit, called "I'll Be Seeing You." Had Mahler written lyrics for Broadway at his mountain retreat, he might have come up with the lines: "And when the night is new / I'll be looking at the moon / But I'll be seeing you."

3

THE ENDLESS ATLAS

Italo Calvino, in his fever-dream novel *Invisible Cities*, imagines a conversation between Marco Polo and the Emperor Kublai Khan. The book is about both the authority and the feebleness of storytelling. The text is divided into fragmentary reports of the cities Polo has visited on the emperor's behalf. The explorer has to convey a sense of the place, with whatever tools are available. One passage from the novel focuses on cartography, at the fulcrum of mathematics and memory: "'I think you recognize cities better on the atlas than when you visit them in person,' the emperor said to Marco, snapping the volume shut." And Polo answers,

> "Traveling, you realize that differences are lost: each city takes to resembling all cities, places exchange their form, order, distances, a shapeless dust cloud invites the continents. Your atlas preserves the differences intact: that assortment of qualities which are like the letters in a name."

Travel is entwined with a search for knowledge, but not only in fact and certainty. It is an epistemic station, somewhere between question and answer, which prizes the in-between above either origin or destination. It isn't enough to simply go about acquiring new information in order to travel. If it were, there might be no meaningful distinction between travel and laboratory science, or studying for a test, or watching the news. Travel is immersive learning of a special kind: in travel we allow ourselves to be surprised, collect new material, catalog and classify at a more intense rate than we might in familiar surroundings. To travel is to revel in discovery itself, in the journey itself.

Consider this analogy from the British philosopher Gilbert Ryle: A mapmaker might come to an ordinary village. The locals know their village perfectly well. They can venture out with perfect confidence that they will be able to get themselves back home. They can negotiate their village with ease; find what they need, visit where they want. They'll have no trouble leading a visitor to the church or the shops. But if you ask the villager to draw you a map or give directions in abstract language, you are asking for an entirely different set of skills. The mapmaker's job is not to teach people how to navigate their own world, but to translate what they know into a system that can be categorized and communicated. A philosopher, Ryle thought, was a mapmaker of language, finding its "logical geography."

Maps are traveling tools. They are small-scale representations of the spatial world, a visual substitute that is comprehensible and digestible. Maps, in their myriad forms, organize our experience, create a material record. The map asks the viewer to see two worlds: the real world around him and the replica, the miniature world in the map. The replica isn't complete (for instance, it doesn't include the viewer looking at the map). As Christian Jacob writes in his book *The Sovereign Map*:

> The map and the library are two aspects of the same project: organizing and codifying knowledge. Both of them rely on accumulation, on tradition, on authority. Some maps could be considered condensed and portable visual libraries, while libraries' catalogs are sometimes organized as a map—a map of culture, of scholarly disciplines, of literary genres. The map and the library are icons of knowledge.

Maps can tell us, in the same spatial idiom, how to find our way home and how to find our way around a place we've never visited before. The code of the map is comprehensible because we already know certain things about the world: we know what it's like to stand next to a river or at the foot of a mountain, or maybe to circle an island in a boat. From there, we can extrapolate some of the bare essentials about any new place. As long as we are on the same planet, in the same dimension of time-space, we can assume a certain number of immutable truths. In other words, if we come to a river or find ourselves on an island, we'll know what to do next.

We tend to think of maps as reasonably stable. We know that maps can change over time, and there is much room for dispute in the allocation of space and status. Post-structuralism has educated us to the power dynamics of mapping, classifications, and the false privilege of nations. Quaint notions of objectivity have largely been banished from most sophisticated quarters. But authority and accuracy are not the only challenges that maps present. Their relationship to reality is much more complex, because their function is even more elemental.

Other conceits of the map we have to accept as abstractions: you may have been to the U.S.-Canadian border, passed through customs, or even gazed through barbed wire, but most borders aren't tangible. Even when they are marked or fortified, they are inescapably arbitrary. They are not real in the same sense that a mountain exists. They are works of fiction. Still, their emotional effect is powerful. We give over an enormous portion of our identity to the stories that these borders tell.

As such, maps tell us an enormous amount about how we see ourselves, and how others saw themselves in the past. Early American maps were drawn with a strong sense of continental thinking. The new country was to be defined by porous borders and open frontiers—just the opposite of the rigid territorialism of Europe. By the 1820s, it was clear that the distinctions between slaveholding and free states would be too great to ignore, and maps started to take interstate borders much more seriously. Maps preserve changing realities for posterity. They tell inconvenient stories.

George Washington owned a map, dated 1755, of the British colonies that included names and territories of Native American tribes. Does it need to be said what happened to those markings on his later maps?

Maps are instruments of power. They tell the stories preferred by the powerful, and they can shape reality. The Radcliffe line, which demarcated the partition of India and Pakistan in 1948, was the creation of British civil servants. There wasn't a cartographer among them, but they created a new political boundary that affected the lives of 88 million people.

The explosion of mapmaking in the fifteenth and sixteenth centuries was a response to the needs of sovereign rulers whose territories had become increasingly large and complex. Maps are a way of staking claims and taking inventory. In *West with the Night*, Beryl Markham writes:

> It seemed that the printers of the African maps had a slightly malicious habit of including, in large letters, the names of towns, junctions, and villages which, while most of them did exist in fact, as a group of thatched huts may exist or a water hole, they were usually so inconsequential as completely to escape discovery from the cockpit.

Mapmakers might stress the apparently insignificant, or at least what seems to them important but has little relevance to anyone else. The villages themselves surely had little interest to imperial mapmakers, but completeness is its own virtue in maps. What can be mapped can be possessed.

All maps tell stories of change and continuity across time. Take a look at the 2012 American electoral map and then look at a Civil War map. Our political identities have adhered to remarkably stable lines. Today, the visual shorthand of Red and Blue America has become a key identity marker on our national topography. It is so pervasive that it's hard to remember that the symbolism is of such recent vintage: during the 1980 election, network television news actually marked the states won by Ronald Reagan in blue. But what do Red and Blue really tell us? To what team should we assign the 44.3 percent of Pennsylvania voters who voted for John McCain in 2008? What about the plurality of El Paso voters who chose Barack Obama? As with most mapping questions, the narrative starts to evaporate the closer you get.

A world map, printed on paper, is an illusion of geometry. In at least one sense, all maps are distorted, because they flatten and delimit spaces that are actually dynamic and endless. Traditionally, maps, like dictionaries, become obsolete the moment they are finished. The paper map freezes the world as it was when the mapmaker created it, as that mapmaker chose to see it. But by the time that map is picked up for the first time by a new viewer, it is no longer a map of the world as it is. This has changed dramatically in the digital age. The Ordnance Society, in the United Kingdom, makes ten thousand changes each day to its maps.

"Now, when I was a little chap I had a passion for maps," recalls Marlow in Joseph Conrad's *Heart of Darkness*. "At that time there were many blank spaces on the earth, and when I saw one that looked particularly inviting on a map (but they all look that) I would put my finger on it and say, 'When I grow up I will go there.'" The blank space on the map suggests the "glories of exploration." The darkness is not ignorance but the grim truth. By the time Marlow was a grown man ready to explore for himself, the "biggest, most blank" spot on the map—Africa—"was not a blank space any more. It had got filled since my boyhood with rivers and lakes and names. It had ceased to be a blank space of delightful mystery—a white patch for a boy to dream gloriously over. It had become a place of darkness."

Heart of Darkness, first published in serial form in 1899, is shaped by a journey into terrible knowledge. The story is well known. A merchant sailor, Marlow, is the pilot of a ship moving upriver in an interior African country—unnamed, but presumed to be the Belgian Congo, where Conrad had been a seaman himself. After a treacherous journey, he arrives at the remote outpost that has fallen under the strange dominion of Kurtz, a cultish figure whose messianic raving ultimately begins to sound saner to Marlow than the cynical double-talk and moral sophistry of the white colonialists.

Raised in Ukraine in an aristocratic Polish family, Conrad's father was a celebrated writer who translated Shakespeare and Dickens into Polish. His mother and father were active in insurrectionist politics against Russian authority. Exiled to the Russian hinterlands, his family suffered terribly for their agitations. Both his parents died young. Though he ultimately wrote in English (he said he was "adopted by the genius of the language"), his first languages were Polish and French, then Russian and Latin.

Conrad was drawn to the sea, which he saw for the first time as a boy near Odessa. He traveled the world with the British merchant navy, where he learned English. Conrad's own experiences in the Congo were transformative. He was "a brute" before he went, he claimed. The misery of colonialism was revealed to him. He learned to be skeptical of what he had been told about Africa, about his home, about the world.

The unusual structure of the book—a secondhand story recounted by a disinterested third party—is one important signal of the book's oblique and complex relationship to knowledge. The anonymous narrator, a sailor who is drawn into Marlow's story without really understanding it, can be a stand-in for a number of things: the unreliable distance between an event and its retelling; the unwillingness of the reading public to look directly at the violence being done in its name. The reader learns almost nothing directly. Much is told but little is explained; in fact, the impossibility of understanding the consequences of the extreme events recounted in the book is the basis of its narrative and moral power. The journey and its interpretation are indivisible. In other words, you really had to be there. We can't know what changed in Kurtz because of what he saw and felt and did in the jungle, nor can we know what Marlow learned when he found him or in the pursuit. In fact, Marlow suggests that the journey changed his very relationship to knowledge. "For a time," he recalls, "I would feel I belonged to a world of straightforward facts; but the feeling would not last long."

The book's climax is an epiphany, voiced by Kurtz in the famous lines, "The horror! The horror!" Marlow calls it "the supreme moment of complete recognition." But, as readers, we don't get to share it. What did he recognize? Kurtz perhaps sees the sham of his "civilizing" mission to Africa. Beneath the pretense—shared with all of Europe at the time—are only greed, cruelty, and animal desire. These are also the last words of a dying man. Though Marlow doesn't understand the content of the revelation, he feels sure that Kurtz has handed down a summary judgment. Maybe this is a natural response to watching a person die: we are so invested in the idea of life, and death, as a journey that we need to feel that a destination has been reached.

Marlow hears in Kurtz "the echo of a magnificent eloquence," but ultimately the acquired wisdom is unnamable. Kurtz's journey had led him to one kind of knowledge, and Marlow had followed him, wanting ever more desperately to know what Kurtz had found at the edge of the river, of civilization, of morality, of humanity itself. Marlow follows him to the edge of the abyss; Kurtz plunges into the void, and Marlow steps back from the edge.

The Nigerian novelist Chinua Achebe, author of *Things Fall Apart*, was a vocal critic of Conrad for many years. To him, Conrad is a racist who could not recognize the humanity in the Africans who populate the story. Africa becomes the Other for Conrad—the representation of a dark and mysterious unconscious and not the home of actual people. The book's stylized impressionism is meant to give the sense that the Africans are incomprehensible and less than human. In an important 1975 essay, he writes:

> *Heart of Darkness* projects the image of Africa as "the other world," the antithesis of Europe and therefore of civilization, a place where man's vaunted intelligence and refinement are finally mocked by triumphant bestiality. The book opens on the River Thames, tranquil, resting, peacefully "at the decline of day after ages of good service done to the race that peopled its banks." But the actual story will take place on the River Congo, the very antithesis of the Thames. . . . We are told that "Going

up that river was like traveling back to the earliest beginnings of the world."

There are many who consider *Heart of Darkness* to be an anticolonial novel, as did Conrad. The book was written in the aftermath of the Berlin Conference, the 1884 summit of colonial powers that carved Africa up among the Europeans. For Achebe, Conrad fails pitifully at any such moral purpose because he does not offer an alternate, holistic representation of Africans. It is not good enough to be a product of one's time, for Achebe, because great artists need to be greater than the times. As Achebe commented in an illuminating discussion with the Caribbean British writer Caryl Phillips, who is far more sympathetic to Conrad:

> No, no. This identification with the other is what a great writer brings to the art of storymaking. We should welcome the rendering of our stories by others, because a visitor can sometimes see what the owner of the house has ignored. But they must visit with respect and not be concerned with the color of skin, or the shape of nose, or the condition of the technology in the house.

Agree or not, Achebe has an important point to make about the limitations of the journey into a foreign land as a quest for self-knowledge. Conrad may have intended the book as commentary on his own society. But, along the way, he encountered a living world that he might not have been equipped to recognize in its fullness and dignity. This is the great danger of treating other people as mere topography.

TRAVEL ENGAGES EVERY SENSE, but there is a reason that "sightseeing" is such a common phrase. Objectivity and observation are both rooted in sight, linguistically and ethically. What we see with our own eyes holds the highest credibility. Sight is also the sense that works from the greatest distance. Touch, taste, smell, and hearing—to various degrees—all require physical proximity. Sightseeing is usually a synonym for tourism, and it is meant to represent the worst of touristic behavior: passive, awkward, insensate, inattentive (the sociologist John Urry described it memorably as the "tourist gaze"). But the act of seeing can also change our understanding of the world in powerful ways.

Travel has shaped the nature of scientific and historical inquiry. Objectivity, that most basic premise of science, is the outsider's advantage. The historian Eric Leed keenly observes that scientific objectivity arises from the disinterested eye of the traveler. What the traveler lacks in interior knowledge, in intimacy and depth, she can only purport to make up for with dispassion and critical distance. This was the unspoken rule of travel writing before the autobiographical turn, sometime in the early nineteenth century. And it has formed the basis for our most robust systems of truth seeking.

Herodotus, writing between 450 and 430 BCE, is often called the father of history. No one believes that history—geological time or even the record of humans—began with him. He is not even credited with producing the first historical record. Thucydides, younger by fifteen years, wrote an account of the war between Athens and Sparta. With his dispassionate tone and political acumen, Thucydides was even closer to a historian in the modern sense. The influential Polish travel writer Ryszard Kapuscinski, whose final book was called *Travels with Herodotus*, put his limitations in perspective:

> He had never heard of China or Japan, he did not know of Australia or Oceania, had no inkling of the existence, much less the great flowering, of the Americas. If truth be told, he knew little of note about western and northern Europe.

Still, he was perhaps the first chronicler of history to explain the world in terms of naturalistic cause and effect, rather than divine intervention. He practiced history as a form of mapping, finding the contours of a place, a people, or a problem through survey and recording. Though he was clear about the distinctions between his work and cartography—and pointedly believed his work to be superior to cartography—he still spent a lot of time thinking about maps and their relationship to space and reality. He writes:

> And I laugh when I see that, though many before this have drawn maps of the Earth, yet no one has set the matter forth in an intelligent way; seeing that they draw Oceanus flowing around the Earth, which is circular exactly as if drawn with compasses, and they make Asia equal in size to Europe. . . . As to Europe, however, it is clearly not known by any, either as regards the parts which are towards the rising sun or those towards the north, whether it be surrounded by sea.

His descriptions of the Greco-Persian Wars are still mesmerizing because he went beyond details of the battle to ask important historical questions about the warring civilizations. Herodotus was born in a Greek city then under Persian rule. His *Histories* intend to recount the past but also to explain it: Why did the Greeks and Persians fight? Why did the Greeks win? Though his methods were limited, he was interested in empirical evidence and was willing to travel in order to collect it.

Herodotus wandered around the Mediterranean and as far as Asia. Travel, in his view, was a tool of history. The chronicle of past events needs to delve into them through the present. He believed in the oral tradition. His journeys involved interviews with witnesses, from leaders to soldiers, from scholars to priests. The result was an engaging composite of viewpoints. He incorporated anecdotes, rumors, and folktales.

Of course, Herodotus, in *The Histories*, could be considered the silent protagonist of his own narratives. His subjective eye weaves the narrative, connecting disparate elements. He is what drives it forward. Not gratuitously, Herodotus was also called, by his critics, "the father of lies," recording events he never witnessed by massaging information gathered from far and wide. Furthermore, he was accused of being biased, an inaccurate chronicler, and, worst, a plagiarist.

The Greek historian Xenophon, in contrast, offered a different type of travel history: simple, direct, straightforward. He was an acolyte of Socrates, leaving us several Socratic dialogues, including the *Symposium* and the *Apology*. But his best writing is found in *Anabasis* ("the journey up," meaning travel to the interior of the country, toward the Black Sea), about his ordeal as a mercenary in the Ten Thousand, an army organized by Cyrus II to take the throne of Persia from his brother Artaxerxes II in 401–399 BCE. Xenophon's interest was in military strategy. But his book is also a study of leadership. And a philosophical disquisition. It is, in the end, a manual of human folly, wherein the author ponders, in his mind, the purpose of it all.

It's hard to imagine a more productive and illuminating trip than Charles Darwin's five years on the HMS *Beagle*. Darwin was only nineteen when he signed up for the voyage and twenty-two when he set sail. He made it onto the ship mostly by good luck. The *Beagle* was a fairly small ship, only about ninety feet long, and packed with seventy-five crewmen. Many officers in the British Navy were amateur naturalists, and it was quite common for seamen to collect samples or specimens for scientific hobbies. The *Beagle*'s captain, Captain Fitzroy, was enthusiastic about the study of weather. Later in life, he would make meaningful contributions to the field of meteorology.

The official purpose of the voyage was to prepare maps. Coastal maps of South America, prepared from information gathered by the *Beagle*, show hundreds of depth readings to help British ships safely navigate coastal areas. Fitzroy wanted the voyage to yield maximum scientific benefits, and he wanted a university-educated man on board for erudite company.

By contemporary standards, Darwin was also an amateur scientist. He had no degree or university position. His work does not much resemble modern scientific writing in form or style. At the time of the trip, he had not even settled on a career in science. He turned down the job at first. His father, who would have to fund the trip, thought it would be an excessive distraction from a meaningful profession. He hoped Darwin would enter the clergy. The trip was also going to be very expensive. Darwin was officially a passenger aboard the *Beagle*. He paid the navy for his meals and hired his own servant. Preparations and additional travel were also costly. In today's money, Darwin's father probably spent well over $1 million. But his father eventually agreed.

Darwin spent about three of the five years on land, collecting specimens of plants and animals that were unknown to science previously. Besides the physical collections, the trip produced insights that Darwin would spend decades unpacking and developing, and which would—it would be no exaggeration to say—fundamentally change nearly every long-held wisdom concerning humankind, the natural world, and the cosmos. He saw evidence of geological processes that challenged the most basic assumptions about the age of the universe. After a devastating earthquake in Chile, Darwin explored the ruin of the city of Valdivia, and he saw in the upturned rock evidence that mountain chains were formed by incremental shifts over eons.

While marveling at the unique platypuses of Australia, so different from anything he had seen elsewhere, he reflected in his *Beagle* diary, "A disbeliever in everything beyond his own reason might exclaim: surely two distinct creators are at work." This was a tentative first step toward a view of the universe that did not depend on the numinous, but could be plotted and understood with human reason. Darwin was creating a new map of reality, which is still being surveyed.

NO MAP CAN be an exact copy of the area it surveys because no map can include everything. In fact, the all-encompassing map is a paradox that has been a common image for describing the limits of knowledge in the face of an infinite and unknowable universe.

Lewis Carroll, in his *Sylvie and Bruno Concluded: The Man in the Moon* of 1889, lampooned the idea of a map with a one-to-one scale. The map was therefore the exact dimensions of the land itself. As it turns out, farmers didn't find it very useful. It covered all the fields and blocked out the sun. So instead they decided to use the territory as the map. "I assure you," Carroll writes, "it does nearly as well."

Jorge Luis Borges wrote a story in 1946 called "On Exactitude in Science." The story was actually inspired by Carroll, elaborating on the joke. It's about an empire whose cartographic ambitions are so grand that nothing can be left unmapped. Like the megalomania and greed of empire itself, the map devours its object and is also devoured by it. The hubris of cartography is its own undoing. The story announces: "In that Empire, the Art of Cartography attained such Perfection that the map of a single Province occupied the entirety of a City, and the map of the Empire, the entirety of a Province." Eventually, the cartographers, dissatisfied as they are, create in Borges's imaginings a map that is, in actual size, the empire itself.

Borges and Carroll, who portray a hunger for knowledge, or at least information, so omnivorous that it can only consume itself, anticipated something of the feeling of saturation, overload, and overconnection that we often struggle against today. David Foster Wallace, a beloved postmodern novelist and for many a prophet of hyperreality, revisited the metaphor in his epic *Infinite Jest* in the mid-1990s. "The world becomes a map of the world," he writes, to describe a kind of low-grade depression—a "spiritual torpor"—in which one loses the ability to feel pleasure or emotional attachment. Appropriate to the era of Prozac, he was describing the world that was becoming more abstract, more hollow, and harder to navigate.

Humans have committed themselves, though later than some would assume, to the symbolic representation of the world. Browse through the past and you'll see one map after another re-creating reality from the vantage point of the present. Today's maps, like Google's, regenerate nearly at the speed of time itself. They aspire to a kind of completeness and omniscience that the most ambitious mapmakers of the past could only fantasize about. We carry them with us, by default, in our phones and GPSs and other devices. They are in motion, as we are, always duplicating the universe on a small scale, easy for us to handle.

The global positioning system (GPS) was conceived in the early 1960s during the Cold War, developed throughout the seventies and eighties, used in commercial aviation in the eighties, and made available to consumers and corporations in the nineties. Around the year 2000, GPS arrived in cell phones. For a while, the U.S. government purposefully interfered with the accuracy of GPS systems. The Cold War giveth and it taketh away. The technology was developed as a result of the West's fear of the Soviets, and also out of that fear the West impeded its further development until after the collapse of the USSR. Today it is basic equipment on nearly any new car. It is used in trillions of dollars' worth of financial transactions that depend on GPS for time stamps.

In one sense, the name "global positioning system" is a misnomer. While it is in fact a global system, and its explicit goal is to cover the whole surface of the earth, it is not the only such global system. GPS is the American system. The Europeans have another system. The Russians and Chinese each have their own systems. Even Japan has a limited network, the only one that is not global by design. Each of these systems would basically be sufficient for everyone, and they all use basically the same technology and radio frequencies. But given how integral GPS has become to the smooth operation of military, economic, and social systems, it stands to reason that none of the major world powers wants to rely wholly on another for this critical service. So the result is a funny paradox: a series of overlapping networks, each global in scope but serving national and regional purposes. It's similar to the paradox we face when we speak of a World Wide Web. It is both an extension and a relic of the space race of the second half of the twentieth century.

There is almost no part of modern life that does not make use of GPS technology. In many cases, whole industries have become dependent. Commercial seafaring now relies totally on GPS, as commercial aviation has for some time. Given its ubiquity and centrality, one would reasonably expect that our GPS infrastructure was robust, redundant, and well secured. But anyone who's actually used GPS, even in your own car or on your own phone, will recognize the truth: the system is actually shockingly fragile. The radio frequencies used by all major systems are surprisingly weak and must travel great distances. In this age of constant vigilance about terrorist threats, it will also naturally occur to us that these indispensable systems are highly vulnerable to mischief. In Britain, officials were perplexed by a proliferation of GPS jamming devices. The problem was getting severe enough that it threatened the basic dependability of the system. After the usual careful study, they found that the culprits tended to be truck drivers whose fleet owners were tracking their vehicles. A simple jamming device was the easiest way to fly under the radar, as it were, long enough for a nap, a detour, or an extra lunch. Authorities also claim to have apprehended terror suspects possessing equipment and plans to disrupt GPS services on a wider scale. The potential effects of such a disruption are far-reaching and catastrophic. There's no need to paint the picture, as most of us have gotten fairly practiced at imagining various technological doomsday scenarios.

Still, the system is fragile enough that it is far more remarkable how little we think about its potential consequences. There are implications both grandiose and banal, both civic and personal. Most drivers with a navigation system in their car have probably had a few near-death experiences just from taking their eyes off the road, remembering their instructions a little too late, but that isn't even the half of it. For those who have become accustomed to these things, it can be unsettling to think about finding ourselves off the satellite grid, without the reassurance of the celestial navigator that knows just where we are and where we're trying to go.

This is a funny thing about technological progress: in solving a problem—that is, making it easier for us to find our way around—we also create a problem that didn't exist before. Before GPS, no one expected to be instantly locatable and to be instantly oriented to our destination. Our previous solution, though not nearly as efficient or technically dazzling, still worked pretty well. We could just find the directions beforehand, and bring a paper map just in case. Now, being cut off from location services provokes anxiety that seems fairly out of proportion to the circumstance. The dead cell phone battery, the dark woods so deep no signal can penetrate: these are well on their way to becoming B-movie clichés, which tells us the fear has penetrated the subconscious. We feel terrified to be alone at moments when we would previously have taken it for granted.

Not that long ago, it took exceptional imagination to envision a world in which each of us has instant access to a global atlas, just by carrying a mobile phone, which would surpass any library in the world. Considering, Carroll and Borges got it nearly right. Except that instead of a master map that covers the whole world, we have an uncountable array of maps, both large and small, which can be customized, personalized, and curated. Our data-gathering ability has grown exponentially in the computer and satellite age.

We are all the center of our own maps. There were times in history when most of the available maps might center on a particular site of power—Rome, Jerusalem, the United States, the USSR. Maps like these certainly still exist. But most of our encounters with maps today start with our present location and display the information we happened to be looking for at the moment. The quest for the perfect map is still very much alive. Today, the gold standard is Google.

Google has been crowing for some time about their ambitions to create a perfect map. Brian McClendon, an executive at Google, wrote a blog post in 2012 and outlined the scope of Google's mapping project. The company, he says, is aiming for nothing less than total comprehensiveness ("We're shooting for literally the whole world," he writes, using an awkwardly imperial figure of speech). And, to be sure, Google has pursued its goal with vigor. They have attached cameras to satellites, cars, jet skis, backpacks. Not only are they dedicated to recording the physical world, they had ambitions to model it virtually. They are now displaying textured 3-D models of entire metropolitan areas, covering the habitats of hundreds of millions of people. In some respects, this is the realization of millions of tiny maps converging into the great map of maps that was once mainly the province of imaginative writers.

And those are just the maps we can all see. Another kind of mapping revolution, fundamentally related and probably even bigger in scale, is going on and almost all of us are both surveyors and surveyed. At every moment, thousands of computers are watching, cataloging, and classifying our interactions with the world. When we purchase something over the Internet, stream a video, look up a restaurant, use a loyalty card, post a picture of our children on Facebook, we are leaving a digital breadcrumb trail. With each transaction or status update, we are filling in details on the map that is being constructed for each of us, and for the truly infinite map of human behaviors for which we are each a crucial data point.

It can be disturbing to think about, but very few people have chosen, or managed, to opt out entirely. Recent revelations about the National Security Agency's surveillance of Americans' phone calls and Internet use have met with some justifiable outrage, though there is little evidence that many people are changing their communication habits. The truth is: we've asked for it. Not only have we consented to it, we've essentially demanded it. We expect most of the services we consume online to be free or nearly free. We expect companies to anticipate our needs and to communicate with us in a personalized way. We get impatient with anything less. In return for all this convenience and personal recognition, we allow ourselves to be mined for useful (and not so obviously useful) information.

As with most things to do with globalization, the costs and benefits of infinite mapping have not reached everyone equally. Many are still waiting and others have fought for their access. In Nairobi, Kenya, dwellers in some of the city's poorest slums took on the task of mapping their own neighborhoods, including informal, semilegal buildings and institutions that don't appear on any official maps, and might never capture the attention of Google's roving eye. They mapped streets without names, schools without addresses, unofficial garbage dumps, and badly neglected roads. Maps have always been contested ground. Recognition on the map is critical to recognition in the world.

Naturally, these developments are impacting the travel and tourism industries. The Internet has already had a major impact on travel, mostly to the benefit of travelers: the ability to search for the best fares for flights or prices for hotels; to preview a show or a restaurant before you visit; to stay connected to home. Now we've entered a new phase, where we each produce vast amounts of data, individually and collectively, and almost all of us carry devices in our pockets that make us easily traceable. The industry sees a lot of value in this. Businesses will pay to know in advance that you're planning a trip to Rome, so they can pitch deals and advertising to you. Companies that once produced travel guides now invite you to leave your own reviews, tips, and images—for free—that they will give away to other travelers, to improve their experience and to generate revenue through page views. Governments will be glad to know who is moving around within their borders. The data you supply will help them decide in advance if you are the kind of visitor they are looking for. The goal, as ever, is to personalize and predict. If the places we go soon start to feel more and more like home, it may be because someone has tried to anticipate our needs and fulfill our data-derived dreams.

For travelers, the instant availability of maps can give us unprecedented freedom to explore new terrain. It's far easier than ever before to make improvisational changes to our itinerary, to find information about a place we've landed serendipitously. In some places, we might be willing to venture a bit farther off the beaten path because we will find it easier to navigate our way back. This is empowering information and access. At the same time, getting off the beaten path is harder than it used to be. Our devices and our connectedness give us support but also impede our adventurousness.

The quest for the perfect map is probably one of those human constants, like our desire for complete knowledge, which is a kind of immortality. The explosion of mapping and data is one of the most significant developments of our time. With it comes danger that we can be lulled into seeing a false wholeness in the world and ourselves. It's easy to think that everything that is to be seen has already been seen. Worse, we might be susceptible to the idea that every place is knowable, every problem solvable, if we just have enough data. If we gather enough tiny bits of information, all the secrets that underlie reality will come clearly into focus. The beauty of discovery has much to do with things out of place, which is something maps cannot afford to tell. Chaos is a constant companion. It always lurks in the background, waiting to redirect our course.

Bruno Latour and Emilie Hermant, in *Paris ville invisible*, write of the map of Paris, "Megalomaniacs confuse the map and the territory and think they can dominate all of Paris just because they do, indeed, have all of Paris before their eyes." Perhaps, but who hasn't felt the reassuring omniscience of looking at the map of a new place and seeing it in front of you? It all looks so comprehensible and surmountable. Every map can seem like an invitation. Likewise, who hasn't seen a map of a familiar place and felt a sense of ownership? Maps, like stories, give us the illusion of a comprehensive view and complete knowledge.

4

THE COSMOS AND
THE CITY

One night, in ninth-century Baghdad—a great setting for a story that is apocryphal but illuminating—the Khalif Al-Mamun was visited by Aristotle in a dream. The philosopher had a message: reason and revelation could coexist; the insights of the Greeks did not conflict with Islam. When he woke up the next morning, he called for the translation of Greek philosophy into Arabic.

Al-Mamun's Baghdad was one of the most prosperous cities the world has ever known. The city was founded around 756 to be the capital and crown jewel of the Abbasid dynasty. By the ninth century, the city had about half a million inhabitants—ten times the size of most European capitals at the time—a scale matched only by Rome and Constantinople. As the seat of an empire that reached from Europe to the Far East, Baghdad was a multicultural city. Persians, Jews, Copts, Berbers, Indians, Greeks, Chinese, and hopefuls from nearly every corner of the world came to try their luck in the big city.

In fact, the translation of Aristotle into Arabic began before Al-Mamun came to power through regicide. But this much is true: in an epoch of prodigious translation, the philosophy, science, and medicine of the ancient world were rendered in Arabic and adapted to Islamic sensibilities. Six hundred years before Aristotle was rediscovered in the West, Arab thinkers were absorbing his texts and reading them in their own language. Though it is conveniently forgotten, it was the preservation of the Greek texts in Arabic that facilitated their translation into Latin a few centuries later—without it there might have been no Renaissance in Europe.

The resources poured into translation at this time are astonishing. Unlike today, translators were very handsomely paid, often on salary. Much of the knowledge accumulated from translation was practical. The field of Islamic medicine is a direct product of the translation movement. In the course of a few centuries, scholars adapted and adjusted the collective medical wisdom of the ancient world. Innovations in science, medicine, and engineering that were contained in the Greek texts were very useful to an ambitious and growing empire. In a world of rival superpowers, all this information was a competitive edge. It was also a potent tool in a war of ideas. The Byzantines may have been Greek, but the real treasures of Greek antiquity were thriving in Arabic. Islam needed to develop a compelling dialectic tradition, a kind of "soft power" that was an important instrument of empire. The Greeks' advanced theories of logic and rhetoric were a valuable curriculum.

"We ought not to be embarrassed of appreciating the truth and of obtaining it wherever it comes from, even if it comes from races distant and nations different from us," wrote the philosopher Ya'qub ibn Ishaq as-Sabah Al-Kindi, in *Fi Hudud al-Ashya Wa-Rusumiha* (On the Definitions of Things and Their Descriptions). Al-Kindi helmed the most famous translation circle. He has been called the first Arab philosopher, building on his deep immersion in the work of Aristotle, as well as an innovator in science, optics, musical theory, chemistry, and a bewildering array of other subjects. He probably didn't speak Greek himself, but he was surrounded by a coterie of mostly Syrian Christians who had fled Byzantine monasteries. The Kindi Circle was an ecumenical and far-reaching network of scholars with facility in Greek, Persian, and Indian sources.

Translation is a peculiar art. Translation is replication, interpretation, and also adaptation. Its closest corollary might be the musician who interprets the compositions of others. To be a faithful interpreter of written music isn't easy; the dedication and talent required is substantial. One has to master the technical demands of the music—but musicians of real distinction also bring something much harder to evaluate, something that shows deep sympathy with the composer and also a distinctive point of view.

The goal of translation is transparency: to be like a pane of glass. Only the imperfections are visible. This is true, but there is another, somewhat contradictory, truth about translation, which captures its special challenge. Edward Sapir, in "The Status of Linguistics as a Science," argues, "No two languages are ever sufficiently similar to be considered as representing the same social reality." To translate a culture is to be able to understand it—but not only that, it is to be able to rearticulate its premises in another tongue. But as Sapir says, there are limits to how completely one can transpose from one language to another. So the translator must capture as much of the original as possible, but must also have the imagination to fill in some of the inevitable gaps in detail, nuance, and sensibility. A synthesis is required. A good translator must know what the words mean, but also know the limits of a language; what can be said, but also what can only be expressed without words and around words.

Sometimes a translator must bridge very different, often divergent worldviews. Kindi and his colleagues had to negotiate some thorny political and theological divisions. The translations themselves would sometimes alter the philosophical content of a source text, as a kind of intellectual diplomacy. The translators, formidable scholars themselves, would write independent treatises to accompany translations. In a translation of the Neoplatonist Plotinus from the Kindi Circle, the translators incorporate a divine "Creator" into the framework of the text, a notion that certainly does not appear in the original. The translation was commissioned by an Islamic empire and most likely translated by a

Christian (with Kindi credited as well). By adding a Creator, the text becomes more palatable to both Christian and Muslim audiences. The German philosopher F. Schleiermacher captures the paradox perfectly in an 1813 lecture, "On the Different Methods of Translation." The translator has only two choices: "Either the translator leaves the author in peace, as much as possible, and moves the reader towards him; or he leaves the reader in peace, as much as possible, and moves the author towards him." This is a difficult choice between competing obligations, and a balance can be struck only with great skill and delicacy.

For modern readers, the kinds of liberties that Kindi took with the Greeks would be a barbaric injustice, especially in the context of an emerging empire looking to co-opt the wisdom of the past to raise its own intellectual profile. But a translator is also a kind of enthusiast, an "evangelical," in Susan Sontag's phrase. This was certainly true for Kindi and his ilk, whatever accommodations they felt were necessary for prevailing moods. The explicit desire is to shape taste, to create access to the work that means most to you, agitating for the significance of a work.

In 1827, Goethe made a bold prediction about the emergence of a world literature, *Weltliteratur*, that would replace the atomized world of discrete local, national literatures. He writes:

> I am more and more convinced that poetry is the universal possession of mankind, revealing itself everywhere and at all times in hundreds and hundreds of men. . . . I therefore like to look about me in foreign nations, and advise everyone to do the same. National literature is now a rather unmeaning term; the epoch of world literature is at hand, and everyone must strive to hasten its approach.

It was the experience of reading literature in translation that opened him up to the possibility, from reading Chinese novels and Persian poetry. He believed adamantly in the capacity of translation, especially in the German language, to give full access to the world of the original.

"World literature" has been a topic of debate since Goethe's time. The long era of nationalism and the nation-state was just getting under way as he made these projections. In the era of globalization and neoliberalism, where nationality is arguably more flexible, the discussion has changed. There are two major factors that drive the conversation today, which are often approached apprehensively: the first, the emergence of a global market for books and international literary celebrity, which depends on translation; the second is the increasing dominance of English as a global language, and the threat it poses to local culture. Tim Parks, in the *New York Review of Books*, captures the concern:

> Perhaps the problem is rather a slow weakening of our sense of being inside a society with related and competing visions of the world to which we make our own urgent narrative contributions; this being replaced by the author who takes courses to learn how to create a product with universal appeal, something that can float in the world mix, rather than feed into the immediate experience of people in his own culture.

As with most conversations about globalization, the real issue is class, not culture. With such a vanishingly small amount of international literature being translated into English, we can now identify a small transnational elite of writers—from Orhan Pamuk to Haruki Murakami to Aleksandar Hemon to Jhumpa Lahiri—who get very wealthy from their writing while most local literatures struggle for viability. While no one could fairly accuse any of these writers of being without culture, or a distinct cultural point of view, there is a sense that some important nuances, some rough edges, have been smoothed out to make the author more palatable to a global audience. While concerns about the hegemony of English are understandable, most of the criticisms miss an important point about many of these writers: they are in fact transnational, to a meaningful degree (Pico Iyer calls it "mongrel fiction"). They live in multiple cultures, move freely, and absorb influences widely. Their status is privileged, for sure, but not necessarily inauthentic.

Still, we hope not to lose the opportunity to read writers—through the great moral endowment of translation—that can also give us access to corners of the world that are not as well covered; which don't merge as smoothly into the multinational stream.

Goethe's ideal of world literature was not particularly egalitarian. German literature was irreplaceably at its center—a "universal possession" of mankind, enriched but never displaced by other cultures. Today it's American culture that represents that central node, globalization's flagship export. Market forces are flattening out the diversity of cultures. Book publishers all over the world compete to acquire local rights to New York Times best sellers. When Dan Brown's latest blockbuster novel, Inferno, was released, a small army of translators in Milan worked around the clock for two months, preparing Spanish, German, Italian, French, and Portuguese editions. They worked in secrecy and under security worthy of the Manhattan Project. Like a major Hollywood film, the book was to be released worldwide on a single day. To date, the author has almost 200 million books in print worldwide.

Understandably, much of the anxiety around world literature is an expression of a deeper discomfort with some of the ways in which the world is changing. Such fears are easily overblown but they are hardly imaginary either. In the developed world, at least, you can easily sense a sort of corporate manifest destiny. Cities, and sometimes countrysides too, have been branded like cattle with the same emblems of Western retail. In a recent science fiction novel called The Fat Years by Chinese author Chan Koonchung, set in a near future in which China has replaced America as universal hegemon, the Wantwant China Group has acquired Starbucks and turned it into an instrument of Chinese soft power, tempting the world with Lychee Black-Dragon Lattes. Though the book addresses many specifically Chinese concerns, it resembles so much postmodern writing from America or England of the last twenty-five years. Its anxieties about globalization, mass culture, and influence are basically the same.

Translation itself is hardly in danger. Governments, business, media, and, of course, travel all depend on translation and interpretation. It is more important than ever, and the practice is changing. Nonhuman translation has major implications for the way we think about language and transmission. Machine translation is a relatively new development, certainly only widely available in the last five years or so. Computers approach translation tasks with the same basic operations as human translation: a text is ingested and processed in a source language; the semantics and grammar of one set of linguistic signs is interpreted and converted into another set; and finally a result is expressed in a new language. Machine translation is, for the time being anyway, always derivative. The machine is only able to survey the accumulated wisdom of humans and the long history of translation. Anyone who has tried to use Google Translate will already know the limitations of what a computer can currently achieve. Tellingly, translation is one area where humans have an unambiguous advantage over machines, which speaks to the immense complexity of the practice.

With so much available to consumers around the world, translation is entering our lives in unexpected ways. While literary translation is still a small field, other kinds of translation efforts have flourished, often with no recognition from scholars, publishers, or other media gatekeepers. There has been, for example, an explosion of fan-generated, crowd-sourced translations for video games, which are now the dominant form of global entertainment (certainly when measured by revenue and participation of young people).

Fascinating translation-based communities have developed to meet the needs of a global consumer base that the major media have not addressed. "Undubbing" is the term for the practice of removing dubbed audio from a foreign video game (usually Japanese) and reinstating the original track, often with English subtitles (this is both a translation movement and an antitranslation movement, at once). As one popular website, Undubbing.com, explains the rationale: "Just like a large number of people prefer to watch foreign films with subtitles in the original language, fans of video games feel the same way about playing their games." This kind of connoisseurship—some would say snobbery—has existed among film buffs for ages. Instead of Truffaut, the favored titles are in the *Final Fantasy* series. While there have always been complaints about low-quality dubbing of television and movies, it is only in the first decades of the twenty-first century that amateur enthusiasts can do anything about it.

To undub video games takes tremendous effort and a fairly broad skill set: multiple languages, programming ability, and so on. The job requires ingenuity and, above all, patience. Often an audio track needs to be manually resynched so that the audio is appropriately timed to the on-screen action. Since these projects are labors of love, the work is often distributed among a global network of fans that meet online and commiserate about particular games. For undubbers, a passion for Japanese culture is an important motivation, as is the desire to consume a more authentic experience. Even for those who are not Japanese speakers—likely the majority of the audience for undubbed media—there is a strong sense that the original dialogue conveys meaning that the translated and dubbed version does not. As Undubbing.com advises sensibly, "The best way to learn a language is to get a good book, download some podcasts, get a conversation partner, travel to the country, work hard, and have fun ;)."

Machine translations and crowd-sourced human translations are in certain respects natural developments in a world that has long depended on translation. They also represent a significant departure. As with many aspects of contemporary culture, the balance of power is shifting away from the autonomous creator: in this case, the translator as auteur.

People are distinguished by their disposition toward language. Some are equipped with a polyglot education. Others live in milieus where multiple languages are constantly in action. That verbal reservoir is useful in travel, for departing from home signifies the secession of language. We'll need to use other words to make ourselves understood.

GOING TO ANOTHER PLACE implies adapting to its idiosyncrasies. These include recognizing that leisure is understood

differently. And so is language. At the heart of travel is the experience of misunderstanding. Can I fit into a rhythm of things that are
unlike my own? And will I be able to communicate with others?
Thus, translation is a requirement, not only between languages
but also between conceptions of time, of space, of culture.

This is particularly clear among anthropologists who travel.
Margaret Mead went to Samoa, where she studied patterns of
behavior different from those in the West. Claude Lévi-Strauss
ventured into Brazil to explore his structuralist view of human
thinking. And Oscar Lewis, prompted by the desire to penetrate
"the culture of poverty," repeatedly interviewed a single Mexican
family to create a composite portrait. Each of these social scien-
tists needed to be equipped with a valise full of knowledge to be
able to comprehend the targeted culture. How do those people see
happiness? What are their basic fears? Are there patterns in their
conduct that are similar to ours and to those of people all around
the world?

Anthropologists are peculiar travelers. They visit a foreign place
time and again until they make themselves at home in it. But in
truth, they are always strangers in it. In fact, the detachment they
arrived with, the detachment they retain, will enable them to see
things scientifically. That is, objectively. Of course, there is no
such thing as objectivity. Yet anthropologists, at least those of
the old school, believed their foreignness was an asset: it enabled
them to see things from the outside. That, they trusted, is the
best way to apprehend the values of a culture.

Translators have the same insider-outsider position. They are
in the know in regard to a social group, but their capacity to speak
to another turns them into bridges. That capacity is essential because translation is also interpretation. Anthropologists are two-
fold translators: they translate from one language to another as
well as from one culture to another.

Mead realized that Samoans have a different understanding
of time because they don't distinguish between work and leisure.
They mate, they hunt, they cook, they interact with one another.
For them the line between the individual and the collective is

nonexistent: the two entities are one and the same. They don't strive to procure satisfaction for themselves alone. And they don't need to rest from what they do, from each other. No such concept exists.

In fact, what distinguished Mead from the Samoans was Mead's curiosity about them. The idea of an outsider spending time with them, befriending them, composing detailed notes about their behavior was bizarre. Why interrupt one's life, why go to such a distance as to abandon one's habitat in order to understand another?

Mead also found that Samoans don't travel. The concept is alien to them. Whoever is part of the community belongs to it in full. When a person dies, she enters another realm, but only then and there and never while still among the living. Intrigued by similar evidence when visiting the Amazon tribes, Lévi-Strauss himself had traveled thousands of miles from his home in France. He needed to learn another set of customs; he forced himself to live in a different habitat. The tribes he describes in *Tristes Tropiques* don't engage in such activity. Their energy is focused on surviving in the jungle, on perpetuating their customs from one generation to the next.

Lewis encountered a different set of rules. His subjects weren't "primitives." Instead, they lived in a working-class neighborhood in downtown Mexico City. The Sánchez family mostly rotated around a commanding father figure. They depended on him for continuity, for financial support, for moral approval. Lewis found some family members leaving the Sánchez household, then coming back after a sojourn. Travel was indeed a component of life. But it was hardly ever about leisure. Most of the time it involved rebellion: confronting the father figure, then running away from him. To be away meant looking for an alternative space, one where freedom seemed at least a possibility. Some members went as far as the United States in search of jobs because they wanted to break away from the cycle of dependency they existed in. In all cases, the anthropologists tell us the story of their encounters with faraway cultures in a language we are able to understand. To do so, they need to translate those encounters into a narrative that suits their readership.

Kindi's claim that we should embrace knowledge wherever we find it, from whomever, seems commonsensical to most modern readers. Certainly, anyone who has an affinity for travel will find it intuitively correct. What's the point of traveling if all the "truth" in the world is already close to home, held among those who look and think like you? To travel, we need to believe we have something to learn; in order to learn new things, we sometimes need to travel.

HUMANKIND HAS REACHED a significant milestone in the twenty-first century: for the first time, more people live in cities than in any other kind of settlement. The city is at the heart of the cosmopolitan experience. At their core, cities are like machines designed for the efficient movement of people. Motion is their reason for being. They are designed to put humans in contact with one another, with as many new people as possible, with maximum opportunities for money and new ideas to spread. The logic of cities is the logic of markets, which is exchange and transmission. As such, they are designed to move people and goods as efficiently as possible from the periphery to the core. They are transportation hubs that deliver new prospects and opportunities from afar and connect to the wider world. They are the customary entry points for immigrants and tourists. They are defined by their capacity to absorb people and ideas. The Norwegian novelist Karl Ove Knausgaard writes in his multivolume autobiographical novel *My Struggle*:

> In the same way that the heart does not care which life it beats for, the city does not care who fulfills its various functions. When everyone who moves around the city today is dead, in a hundred and fifty years, say, the sounds of people's comings and goings, following the same old patterns, will still ring out.

Cities are complicated places that make simple identification more difficult. After World War II, Hungarian right-wingers gave

Budapest a strange name: the Guilty City. What crimes can cities commit? For the nationalists, the city was an offense against their sense of what it meant to be a Hungarian. This is why the cosmopolitan promise of cities is so potent and threatening to those who prefer the boundaries between people to be clean, simple, sanitized. Just as cities have always been places where disease could spread with chilling efficiency—why the wealthy have often retreated to the countryside for the summer, a legacy of the age of plagues—it is impossible to prevent the viral movement of people and ideas. Cities are impure. They are contaminated.

Even in our increasingly virtual world, cities have not lost their magnetism. If anything, they have emerged stronger than before, after a long period of decline when it was not uncommon for serious people to ask if cities had any future at all. Today, major global cities are becoming increasingly focused on supporting the lifestyle aspirations of the elite. New York, London, Paris, Moscow, Tokyo, and Sydney have become unattainable to all but the wealthiest (as Rebecca Solnit writes in *A Book of Migration*, "Wealth destroys cities in ways that poverty does not"). Though cities vary enormously around the world, the major global cities increasingly follow a certain pattern: a privileged core that the most prosperous locals share with tourists; as you leave the center, the fortunes start to thin out and the visitors mostly disappear; at the edges are the poorest and usually most recent arrivals.

Cities have a hold on the imagination because they give us a place to lose ourselves, to reinvent ourselves, to try on different ways of living. Cities are also the hodgepodge of humanity: all walks of life coalesce in them. Their coexistence creates the impression of an endless human whole, a sum of parties. Cities aren't only spaces of cohabitation but states of mind. In the city we learn to share our uniqueness. In the city we enter a whirlpool whereby what we bring and what others bring creates a mosaic. And it keeps changing. Its past is renewed, always shedding elements, constantly adding new ingredients.

Cities distill knowledge in both deliberate and haphazard ways. That's how the city works: as organized chaos, or else as chaotic organization. Their monuments memorialize the past. Their government buildings distill power. Layers of history are accumulated on each block. Cities are designed to allow visitors in, to allocate their curiosity in productive ways.

THE TERM "COSMOPOLITAN" comes from the Greek words *kosmos* (universe) and *polis* (city): it means a citizen of the world. Is it really possible to be a citizen of the world? Is that not a contradiction in terms? At the least, it is meaningfully paradoxical. Citizenship does imply affiliation with a specific and defined group; that it is specific and defined suggests that, by necessity, it also excludes. The boundaries of obligation conferred by citizenship are defined just as much by who is outside the line as by who falls within. So that contradiction is meant to signal an imaginative leap beyond our ordinary conceptions of responsibility and belonging.

The Roman playwright Terence wrote, "I am a human being, I consider nothing that is human alien to me." Karl Marx once posed the phrase as a personal maxim on a "Confessions questionnaire" (the Victorian equivalent of a yearbook quote or a Facebook profile).

Terence was a citizen of the Roman Republic, but of North African descent. He was possibly born to a slave or was himself brought to Carthage as a slave from what is now Libya. From his vantage, his universalist attitude was both magnanimous and self-preserving. For someone born a slave, or born to slaves, affirming your humanity—and claiming that your humanness is your most important characteristic—is a bold and necessary step.

The Stoics, who emerged in third-century Athens—and who gave shape to our understanding of cosmopolitanism—described themselves as "human beings living in a world of human beings and only incidentally members of polities." The Stoics believed that humans lived their lives in two overlapping realms: local and cosmic. Like liberal nationalism, cosmopolitanism is an individualist tradition. Both include a deep conception of mutual obligation. In neither case is the value of a human person separate from her relations to others. For cosmopolitans, every individual, regardless of location or status, is valued for the humanity she shares with all other humans. In other words, everyone in the world is like me—even as I respect or celebrate diversity, I believe that what every person has in common with me is more consequential than the arbitrary details that mark our differences.

"Cosmopolitan" has had many meanings over time: some noble but some deeply ugly, like the coyly anti-Semitic "rootless cosmo-politan." The implication is clear enough. Cosmopolitanism has no inherent moral connotation. The ability to transcend national boundaries is not, in itself, a moral proposition. Multinational cor-porations are cosmopolitan; so are empires. The slave trade was cosmopolitan in a sinister sense, as is high-seas piracy.

At least since the time of the Greeks, there have been people who expected that the emancipation of individuals from fixed identities and social positions would lead to a world in which nar-row associations would be less significant. Political membership would gradually incline toward larger and more inclusive groups. During the Enlightenment, thinkers from Voltaire to Leibniz felt assured that all signs pointed toward an emerging cosmopolitan order.

Needless to say, reality has not moved in this direction. First, nation-states, which Enlightenment thinkers could only dimly anticipate, proved to be a resilient form of political order. Second, the individualism trumpeted during the Enlightenment did not lead to a "flatter" version of personal identity; on the contrary, it brought a demand for recognition of particularism and attach-ments, for the right to express the "authentic" inner being. In Cat-alonia, Quebec, and Scotland, there are independence-separatist movements today that passionately wish to subdivide further, who feel that the current configurations of nations don't give adequate recognition to their ethnic and historical identities. Though usu-ally dismissed as eccentric today, such national movements were extremely important to decolonization across the globe in the twentieth century. The desire for national recognition has become, in the modern parlance of human rights, an inalienable expression of human dignity.

With the upsurge of global communication, a constant barrage of images increasingly defines our perception of the world. They come to us from TV, in movies, over the phone, and online. These images create a bizarre illusion of time and space: we all seem to be, in some sense, intimates; what happens in one place affects what happens everywhere else. But the simple conviction that we are connected by life on a shared planet is disingenuous. There is almost no one who really thinks of the world in this way. To most people, our globe might look more like two, or three, or four worlds: the rich at the top, the poor at the bottom; we divide the world geographically—the Northern and Southern Hemispheres, the civilizational divide between East and West. The North is a place of bounty with plenty of happiness to go around, for the right price; the South deprived, depraved, corrupt. Likewise, the West is rational, coherent, and individualistic, whereas the East is fanatical, impulsive, and dangerous.

Like those who once believed that world governance was just around the corner, idealists of universalism tend to overestimate people's willingness to relinquish their specific identities—or their willingness to extend human dignities to others. What we have instead is a world where capital moves freely, where the wealthy travel with ease and the poor are easily moved along. Brands may be global, but politics remain local. Governments act transnationally when it is profitable, and speak like nativists when it's popular.

Similar overoptimistic predictions have been made about the impact of travel. It has often been predicted that tourism would lead to erosion of borders. Tourists would travel to distant lands and see the folly in dividing people along arbitrary political lines. This was far too hopeful. We certainly think about borders differently today. Many borders have become porous. Imagine telling a Polish person in 1962 that one could drive from Warsaw to Paris today almost without interruption (other than traffic). A black South African can move more or less freely around Johannesburg today. At the same time, new borders have been erected and some old ones are more impenetrable than ever.

For travelers, the world is far more open than it has been at any point in history. More people have access to travel, people can move around with far greater ease, and more societies are willing and even eager to play host. Of course this is not true everywhere. There are plenty of places that are far more dangerous or inhospitable than they were a generation or even half a century ago.

You certainly don't need to be a cosmopolitan to travel, but travel is an expression of cosmopolitan impulses. If a person believed that the world was truly flat, but the differences among humans were all incidental or accidental, there wouldn't be much reason to travel. One would only expect to find new destinations that closely resemble home. So travel requires that we take our differences seriously. The Ghanaian-British philosopher Kwame Anthony Appiah defines a modern cosmopolitanism as "universalism plus difference." Even if we are part of the same moral community, and our basic obligations extend to all other humans, we can still relish the diversity we find in the world. When we travel we seek it out. We are stepping into unfamiliar terrain, into the domain of the Other precisely so that we can see the world from her vantage. We are exploring what is durable in our bonds to strangers and we are also looking to experience the novelty and divergences in other people's realities.

The moral challenge of the cosmopolitan is to entertain competing, often contradictory, ideas about what is good and right, or what is true, or even what is interesting or beautiful. Even if we believe in the common humanity, a person would have to be willfully blind to miss the fact that people express their humanity in a bewildering variety of ways. Some of these differences are small, even superficial. It is not a moral quandary to recognize that different people like to dress differently, enjoy music that may sound strange to another person, or even enact their religious devotions in diverse ways. None of us should find these differences threatening. They are only to be celebrated, engaged with curiosity, respected.

But of course not every difference we encounter can be met with equanimity. In Saudi Arabia, women are not allowed to drive cars.

In parts of Latin America, Africa, India, and elsewhere, young girls are forced into marriage. Around the world, children are pressed into military service or gangs. As much as 40 percent of the Bolivian army is under eighteen. In Chechnya in the early 2000s, children as young as eleven were recruited by separatist forces and sent to the front lines. Any moral code worthy of the name must allow us our outrage and horror at such facts, without demonizing or dehumanizing large groups of people or sliding into feckless relativism. These are only the most extreme examples; there are countless small and large contentions that divide peoples and cultures and worldviews. In a heterogeneous country like America, the spectrum of mainstream creed is relatively narrow when it comes to governance (Democrats and Republicans are not so terribly far apart on the basics of political power). But Americans are wildly divided on other fundamental issues, like abortion or the origins of the universe.

Traveling to unfamiliar places or among people that seem dramatically different from us—this could be Algeria or Alabama—we can find ourselves in some delicate situations where the right thing to do, ethically or socially, is not always obvious. We often have to make concessions to the customs of our host, small and not so small. Sometimes a vegetarian will eat pork so as not to seem ungrateful. Sometimes a staunch feminist will cover her head before entering a place of worship to respect local norms. These are perfectly respectable choices, just as it would be reasonable to politely refuse the meat or choose not to visit the place where the customs were objectionable to you. These moments can be awkward but, in a way, these aren't terribly hard decisions. Mostly it comes down to good manners and personal conscience. Hopefully you wouldn't choose to lecture or protest, which should seem like a good idea to no one. And hopefully you won't make a choice that you would deeply regret later, feeling that you had compromised a core belief for the sake of decorum.

In most cases like these, live and let live is ethical guidance enough. To behave is the easy part. What's more challenging is to accept the limitations of our own beliefs. To experience other people without fear or condescension. It is unrealistic, and frankly un-cosmopolitan, to expect that we can resolve all disagreements of such far-reaching significance. Cosmopolitanism permits us to share basic human experiences while still being rooted in our own time, place, and perspective.

We hear a lot about how Americans have sorted themselves along ideological and cultural lines. We are less likely to have neighbors with opposing views, we consume our media from sources that reinforce our biases, and we are less likely to interact with people from different socioeconomic backgrounds. If this is so—as it seems to be for many—travel then becomes an even more necessary tool for encountering new ideas, influences, and prospects. It is also a reminder that we need to bring some of the virtues of travel and cosmopolitanism back into our daily lives. In "Debits and Credits," Rudyard Kipling wrote:

All good people agree,
And all good people say,
All nice people, like Us, are We
And everyone else is They:
But if you cross over the sea,
Instead of over the way,
You may end by (think of it!) looking on We
As only a sort of They!

PART II

How We Travel

5

THE SERIOUS BUSINESS

OF LEISURE

In his essay "Self-Reliance," Ralph Waldo Emerson writes that "he who travels to be amused . . . travels away from himself." The word "travel," as is often noted, shares its root with "travail." For most people this would seem foreign to their experience of travel, which we now associate mostly with pleasure. There are still inconveniences and hassles and occasional risks—all multiplying as our choices of destinations get more exotic and ambitious. But, ultimately, most of our travels are for the purpose of diversion or enrichment.

In contrast, the word "tourism" is difficult to define, not because the activities are hard to recognize, but because it's nearly impossible to give a simplistic account of its opposite, what it is not. If travel is defined, at least in part, by hardship, then tourism must be fairly effortless; it must be travel without trial, what we usually call leisure. But that raises as many questions as it answers. In fact, leisure is an important place to start, because "travel for leisure" at least gets us on the road to defining tourism.

Leisure is, like travel, most easily understood in relation to what it is not: labor, ardor. Leisure is the absence of work, of compulsory activity. When we aren't working, we are at ease. And if we're at ease, we're free, or so is the impression. But this only gets us so far in the context of travel, partially because these ideas are so subjective. Leisure is a species of pleasure, though it is not synonymous with pleasure. There are many pleasurable experiences that are not leisurely. And there are leisure activities that are not necessarily pleasurable. This is particularly true for leisure travel, which presupposes certain preference that are, by no means, universal: a Caribbean resort is hardly an ordeal, but it is not everyone's idea of fun. New Year's Eve in Times Square is unmistakably a tourist experience, but it is hardly relaxing. Nor is bungee jumping.

Every society we know of has outlets for noncompulsory, nonremunerative pursuits. Leisure is a serious topic in the history of thought, connected intimately with the search for a meaningful life. In the *Nicomachean Ethics*, Aristotle writes that "happiness is thought to depend on leisure; for we are busy that we may have leisure, and make war that we may live in peace." Leisure is the end goal of labor; labor is the price we pay for leisure, including the freedom to pursue contemplative activities. Leisure is a thing of inherent worth—uniquely so, even. By such a standard, the casual and common uses of the word—and its associations with frivolity and indulgence—seem impoverished.

Aristotle distinguishes leisure from play, mere recreation. Play, in fact, "belongs to the sphere of work," he wrote in *Politics*, "for he who works hard needs rest and play is a way of resting." Leisure, on the other hand, is "in itself a pleasant, happy existence which the life of work and business cannot be." Leisure is not a respite from effortful work; leisure is an encounter with the intrinsically good, the fundamentally and definitely human. It is the essence of *eudaimonia*, the Greek word for human flourishing, which requires the leisurely cultivation of perfect, rational thought. (The Greek word for leisure is directly related to the English word "school.") This is the life of contemplation, cognition—and the freedom they afford, as well as the freedom necessary to achieve them.

The relationship between these opposites is thus dialectical, much the same way as when we say that for happiness to exist, there must be misery; and for joy to manifest itself, sadness must recede. That is why sometimes the definition of one of these conditions presupposes the negation of the other: happiness is the absence of misery. Leisure only comes when we aren't working, just as travel takes place when we aren't standing still.

Leisure, then, is freedom because work is imprisonment. But if leisure is the escape from (the negation of) prison, from what does it free us? Aristotelian leisure requires the kind of discretionary time and material ease that only come with privilege. This kind of leisure is intended strictly to relieve certain types of people from the duties that burden most other people. Aristotle thought of leisure as a state conducive for mental discipline. Pierre Bourdieu, in *Pascalian Meditations*, captured the contemplative value of leisure thus: "the free time, freed from the urgencies of the world, that allows a free and liberated relation to those urgencies and to the world."

In the nineteenth century, Karl Marx and Friedrich Engels envisioned an unfettered life in which, as Marx put it, one could "hunt in the morning, fish in the afternoon, rear cattle in the evening, criticize after dinner . . . without ever becoming hunter, fisherman, herdsman or critic." This would sound more like work than recreation to most contemporary readers, as it probably did to both Marx and Engels. What they are describing is really the absence of professionalization; people can participate in various types of labor without being defined by them. This is a compelling vision of leisure as freedom, but it doesn't include the freedom from labor. It is freedom from coercion.

For a thinker so easily caricatured for his obsessions with production and work, leisure is a serious topic for Marx. Leisure is also a form of production, part of self-realization and development, and a superior mode to labor, at that. With his deep roots in romanticism and Enlightenment ideas, he believed in a fundamental human relationship to nature, with which "humanity must remain in constant exchange."

Labor under capitalism has turned the self—both body and spirit—into a commodity. Even nature itself becomes an instrument. We become alienated from ourselves by coarse materiality, when our hard work creates no meaning in our own lives and only enriches others. Labor is an essential part of human experience, and a productive force. Marx's leisure is not idleness and it is not—as, again, in the caricature—an entitlement. Leisure is the goal of labor, as peace is the goal of war. As the Marxist philosopher Raymond Williams put it in an essay titled "Work and Leisure," published in *The Listener* on March 25, 1961, "In leisure . . . we feel for the time being that our life is our own." To work means to be slave of someone else's rule and to be at leisure means to be one's own sovereign.

Once there was something called the leisure class, and its meaning was broadly understood. The sociologist Thorstein Veblen coined the term at the end of the nineteenth century. In his critique, he defined leisure as the "nonproductive consumption of time." The leisure class was exempted by their privilege from industrial labor and social utility. Veblen was American-born, of Norwegian extraction. In the last decade of the century, he watched as industrialists like John D. Rockefeller amassed personal fortunes previously unknown in the New World. A new American aristocracy was exploding into being. In this new class he saw a relic of European-style feudalism.

The members of this class were mainly interested in reinforcing and projecting their own status, while the rest of society generated wealth and did useful things. Veblen writes in *The Theory of the Leisure Class*:

> The institution of a leisure class is the outgrowth of an early discrimination between employments, according to which some employments are worthy and others unworthy. Under this ancient distinction the worthy employments are those which may be classed as exploit; unworthy are those necessary everyday employments into which no appreciable element of exploit enters.

Veblen's leisure class is parasitic, insular, equipped for leisure only. It's defined by "conspicuous exemption from all useful employment." The underlying scandal of the evolution of a leisure class is that labor and leisure are inverted in value. Instead of venerating productivity, the leisure class anathematizes it.

The relationship between work and leisure today is more complex. Leisure is no longer the exclusive property of an elite. Instead, it has been both democratized and commodified. In many respects, as leisure no longer signifies exclusivity and privilege, the superrich have ceded it to the middle and upper-middle classes. By most accounts, individuals with the highest net worth in developed countries are now likely to work far more hours per week than those who earn less. The culture of achievement that pervades most Western societies makes few allotments for discretionary time. Indeed, we pride ourselves on the density of our calendars, our multitrack attention, our permanent connectivity and availability. Ironically, where success was once identified with leisure, it is now far more identified with work. According to the *New York Times*, the top 1 percent of American earners is three times more likely to work more than fifty hours per week. The psychologist Daniel Kahneman, in an article in the *Washington Post*, argues that "being wealthy is often a powerful predictor that people spend less time doing pleasurable things and more time doing compulsory things and feeling stressed."

We have erased many of the borders between work and leisure. Learning is playing, playing is thinking, thinking is working, working is learning. We turn gratification into a moral obligation: we encourage young people to follow their heart, to pursue their dreams, to make a fixation of inspiration and fulfillment. In an influential essay called "Free Time," Theodor Adorno decries a kind of ersatz freedom, part of a spell that capitalist societies cast over citizens, dulling their sense of the system's inherent brutality. Influenced by Marx's diagnosis of a commodity fetish, Adorno believed that real leisure, which is a way of life, has devolved into free time, which is really just an extension of labor: "What happens at work, in the factory, or in the office can only be escaped from by approximation to it in one's leisure time." Instead of leisure, we consume the banal products of the "culture industry."

He defended the seriousness of his nonwork pursuits, refusing to devalue their significance:

> I have no hobby. Not that I'm a workaholic who wouldn't know how to do anything else but get down to business and do what has to be done. But rather I take the activities with which I occupy myself beyond the bounds of my official profession, without exception, so seriously that I would be shocked by the idea that they had anything to do with hobbies. . . . Making music, listening to music, reading with concentration constitute an integral element of my existence; the word hobby would make a mockery of them.

The degrading slide from culture to commodity, from leisure to free time, from authenticity to phony reproduction—described with such visceral disgust by Adorno—is similar to the way many have described the transition from travel to mass tourism. Instead of a challenge, tourism promises diversion. Adorno, in an essay called "Enlightenment as Mass Deception," writes:

> Amusement under late capitalism is the prolongation of work. It is sought after as an escape from the mechanised work process, and to recruit strength in order to be able to cope with it again. But at the same time mechanization has such power over a man's leisure and happiness, and so profoundly determines the manufacture of amusement goods, that his experiences are inevitably after-images of the work process itself.

As with so many other things, we have shifted our idea of leisure from an ethical or objective reality to a matter of self-actualization and subjective experience. Leisure is a way of describing those activities that we pursue outside of our working life. It is an emotional release that is necessary for psychic balance and wellness. It is a state of mind, which is to say, it is in the realm of psychology and belief. The social psychologist John Neulinger, a preeminent theorist of leisure, writes in *The Psychology of Leisure*, "Leisure is a state of mind; it is a way of being, of being at peace with oneself and what one is doing." Neulinger's theory of leisure is based on two criteria: that one engages willingly with the activity, and that is pursued for its intrinsic worth. He also predicted a world that was tilting toward greater leisure, where the concept of a job would seem anathema, where nonleisure work would be at best a minimal aspect of daily life.

NEW ATTITUDES TOWARD work and leisure are usually leading indicators of big cultural shifts. The things we do with our leisure time—what we do for fun, or because we believe it is important—says a lot about who we think we are and how we want to relate to society. We identify strongly with our work, as with our hobbies and personal passions. This is another way in which work and leisure are mirrored. Both are strongly associated with self-actualization.

Wealthy Americans in the nineteenth century, like their counterparts in Europe, had a reasonably well developed tradition of leisure. They went to spas and baths. They traveled for pleasure. At the time, it was really only the wealthy who could travel for pleasure, because they had the means to ameliorate the difficulties of travel.

By midcentury, as trains became more pervasive, opportunities for travel with leisurely intent began to trickle down to the middle and working classes. Besides improved transportation, there was also a growing population of urban professionals who started to live by a calendar more conducive to vacation. These were also among the first American workers to enjoy a luxury that would soon be taken for granted, though less so today: the paid vacation. At the time, conventional scientific thinking was that workers without breaks could suffer "brain fatigue." Time off became a health imperative. This consideration wasn't extended to the working class until the Progressive Era.

Always ambivalent about idleness, Americans worked hard at vacation, creating a new kind of recreational culture and economy. An industry developed to meet the demands of this emerging middle class that now had some time on their hands, a little disposable income, and a reasonably comfortable way to move around the country.

American tourism has embodied the twin impulses of self-gratification and industriousness. Even today, both concepts of leisure coexist: the restorative and the edifying. Cruise lines offer lectures on anthropology and art collecting. Colleges offer summer institutes, with illustrious guest instructors and plenty of time for tennis.

To vacation is to leave behind the routine. In other English-speaking countries, people might "go on holiday," but Americans "take vacations." The time we take for travel, or even other time away from work, is something Americans must seize. Part of the thrill of vacation is that we are leaving something behind, shirking some responsibility (even if by previous arrangement). For a culture so preoccupied with autonomy and ownership, *taking* a vacation is to *take back* some portion of the freedom that has been forfeited in the name of employment. It's perfectly emblematic of American ambivalence about identity and work. On one hand, we get strong messages from the culture that our professional self is our most important self. We are what we do. In fact, the most innocuous and ubiquitous question—"What do you do?"—is another revealing American idiosyncrasy. Almost any American would recognize that the question is an invitation to announce your professional identity. Even though answers like, "I like to play tennis" or "I build model airplanes" or "I often drink too much" are perfectly logical responses to the question, as formulated, they are clearly wrong.

How we think about work and leisure is also symptomatic of how we think about authority. In the 1960s, the revolt against middle-class professionalism took the shape, in the popular imagination at least, of the commune. This was the pinnacle of the counterculture's radical critique of mainstream America. "Tune in, turn on, and drop out" was a protest against a certain ideal of work even more than an embrace of drugs. The same could be said of the kibbutz and other socialist experiments in reimagining—and harmonizing—economic and cultural life. Creating a new culture starts with changing the way members relate to work.

Today, it is the start-up. Like the commune, it is another response from youth culture to bourgeois expectations. The media refrain of "disruptive technologies" implies a revolutionary shift that will transform lives, or at least businesses. The commune and the start-up both involve hard work. Both are revolts, not against work but against the conformity of professionalization, which is a capitalist society's most potent form of socialization. The start-up and the commune both package work, often very traditional in nature, in the aesthetics of leisure. The conceit is: we can own our work without submitting to authority; we can be successful without the hierarchies, the mercenary capitalism, the social compliance. Either a commune or a start-up is capable of producing genuine, meaningful innovation (in product and process, but almost never in politics or civic life; in most instances, they are similarly antipolitical). Still, most outsiders will identify them first by their audacious informality—from casual sex to casual Fridays.

As with many other innovations in lifestyle and commerce, America's postwar economic expansion created an unprecedented appetite for leisure. Perhaps for the first time, leisure came to be seen as a viable way of life, if not life's purpose. This is the concept of leisure at its most democratic and also its most mercantile.

Appropriately, California was at the vanguard. The growth of Los Angeles and Southern California, from a frontier with few natural resources to a world capital of escapist culture, was built on a promise and a brand rooted in leisure. Before this westward expansion, the typical Anglo-American view of leisure was deeply equivocal. Leisure was something to be enjoyed briefly, a diversion from meaningful work, a recuperative intermission. The nineteenth-century Anglo settlers who first visited California were taken by the apparent simple effortlessness of Spanish-Indo-Mexican culture. Some voiced concerns that, preposterous though they may be, haven't totally left us; they worried that white Americans would be infected by Mexican laziness.

The people who built Los Angeles were selling something different. And they weren't just selling vacations, though tourism played an outsized role in the economic development of the region. They didn't have a great port or a natural industrial base. In fact, even the natural environment itself, though beautiful and alluring, also had many inhospitable features and environmental hazards. But they also had sunshine. They had the beach. Of course, people in California would have jobs, responsibilities, hardships. But just living in Southern California came with a promise of recreation, relaxation, and health. As it is everywhere else, someone's leisure is another person's labor. But in Los Angeles, leisure was seen to be in the very DNA of the place, and even the working classes could enjoy the weather, might even be able to afford a backyard pool.

A man named Charles Fletcher Lummis was an important early booster for the California way of life. He understood that Los Angeles would sell leisure to the world. It could be a destination for tourists and transplants. He seemed to intuit that the city's special genius would be to redefine the good life for a global audience. He certainly had the requisite showmanship. He arrived in Los Angeles on foot, walking all the way from New England—a clever publicity stunt. His message was audacious and sensational: not only was this a new frontier of land, but it was also an evolutionary leap for humankind. His book *A Tramp across the Continent* was meant to illustrate, as Phoebe Schroeder Kropp put it in *California Vieja: Culture and Memory in a Modern American Place*, "the growth of Man in the New World from savagery to highest civilization." This association of civilization and pleasure was not new, but in California it was taken to a great extreme and everyone was (theoretically) invited to the party.

In Roman Polanski's classic film *Chinatown*, Los Angeles is the star player in all its mystery and fragility. Early in the film, a developer reminds a town hall audience of the precariousness of their city: they live on the ocean, but also at the edge of the desert. The film was inspired by California's water wars in the early twentieth century, when water was diverted from farmland to the unquench-able city. In the film's exquisite cinematography, water is a critical motif. It projects abundance, but also artifice, like the fake ponds that appear as settings throughout. Visually, it expresses perfectly the very improbability of the place, this city built on fantasy and salesmanship.

In many respects, this was the beginning of the next phase of the leisure industry, going far beyond what Europeans had known. This was the vacation that never had to end. Lummis, who was also the editor of the magazine *Land of Sunshine* (later called *Our West*), wrote, "Southern California was destined to show an astonished world the spectacle of Americans having a good time."

AN ENTITY CALLED the World Leisure Organization (WLO) has existed since the early 1950s. In the mode of the World Travel Orga-nization (which is a United Nations body while the WLO is not), it has a charter that is steeped in the language of international human rights norms. Read the charter of the WLO and you'll be mesmer-ized. Article 1, often quoted, states unequivocally, "All people have a basic human right to leisure activities that are in harmony with the norms and social values of their compatriots. All governments are obliged to recognize and protect this right of its [*sic*] citizens."

Most people today would agree that freedom of movement is a basic right, or would uphold that a person should not be pre-vented from traveling. Does that also mean that a society has an affirmative responsibility to provide opportunities for leisure? There is something unseemly about a trade lobby group deploy-ing such moralism, especially when their morals are so favorably correlated to their business interests. After all, leisure cannot be imposed: it must be individually sought; otherwise it isn't a by-product of freedom. What kind of leisure activities could qual-ify as basic human rights? If we frame it as a negative injunction, that a society should not preclude citizens from the recreational enjoyments of their choice, then it sounds fairly uncontroversial. Arthur Frommer, the impresario of postwar American guidebooks, has made the argument that our right to travel should go far beyond our current debates over paid vacations. He starts an opinion piece by saying, "Although there isn't the slightest chance that the current Congress will pass such legislation, I continue to yearn for the day when we as a nation will assist the poor to travel." In laissez-faire America this does sound rather fanciful. But his argument is reasonably sound on fairness grounds:

> When the non-poor travel, who pays for the highways on which they drive their cars? Who funds the aviation authorities that secure the safety of their landing fields and flight paths? Who maintains the port facilities, docks and marinas at which they park their boats? Because the taxpayer is already so heavily supporting travel by middle-income and high-income Americans, common justice requires that at least some resources be spent on travel by the poor. Call me a stargazer, but I believe in "social tourism." And someday we'll follow the lead of the several European countries that have adopted at least some measures of tourism for the poor.

Frommer, naturally, also has a commercial interest in expanded access to travel. Such enlightened public policy can have an enormous impact on tourism revenue. France, in particular, which was the first country to legislate for paid vacations, is still the world's leading tourism destination, receiving more travelers annually than even the United States. As a result, hospitality is the country's biggest industry and employer. In the wake of the 2008 financial crisis, a robust tourism sector helped keep France, and much of Europe, afloat as unemployment soared across the continent.

Travel, of course, doesn't require leisure to be liberating. Human mobility of nearly any kind—with obvious and ugly exceptions, such as human trafficking or forced migration—holds the possibility of certain kinds of freedom. We have the opportunity to escape familiar social expectations, routines, or sanctions. To try on new personas, remake our lives, pursue other opportunities, and adopt new modes of experience. But leisure, of one kind or another, is a necessary part of tourism.

Turning leisure into travel requires an inversion of means and ends: travel for leisure purposes, such as relaxation, enlightenment, and edification, involves more than the imagination. It needs time, energy, and resources. For the purposes of defining tourism, what leisure means is far less important than who pursues it.

6

TRANSPORTED

"Flying to me isn't travel," Paul Bowles said in a 1981 interview with the *Paris Review*. "Flying is like television: you have to take what they give you because there's nothing else." Known for novels about itinerant protagonists in search of ephemeral truths, Bowles believed travel expired with the steamship.

Bowles speaks of it in the past tense, with an air of lament, impossible in the age of rapid transit and all-inclusive vacation packages. But if travel is over, then what is tourism, which is a fixture of modern life in nearly every corner of the world, and which thrives as perhaps the world's biggest business—and which continues to reshape the global terrain of culture, ecology, and commerce?

Travel has been declared dead—or dying—many times, especially by those who see themselves as above mere tourism. In Bernardo Bertolucci's film adaptation of Bowles's 1949 novel, *The Sheltering Sky*, which is the story of a wealthy American couple who are traveling somewhat listlessly through North Africa, the distinction between a tourist and a traveler is a psychic wedge between the protagonists that unfolding events will soon exploit. As the wife tells her husband, with lavish condescension that implies she is speaking only of herself, "We're not tourists, we're travelers. . . . A tourist is someone who thinks about going home the moment they arrive, whereas a traveler might not come back at all."

This is, needless to say, setting the bar rather high. If this is what is required of a traveler—essentially, to walk up to the brink of self-exile, to be willing to abandon any obligation or commitment, to have no attachment to any home worth upholding—then it hardly seems like an honorific worth having at all. But there is an enduring appeal to the identity of a traveler—even if we only slip it on recreationally or sporadically—that clearly speaks to something powerful in our self-conception. At the same time, tourists are everywhere, and we have probably all been tourists at least a few times in our lives, though you'll likely never meet someone who describes herself as such. Everyone considers herself a traveler—and we are all surrounded by tourists.

In the seventeenth and eighteenth centuries, the sons of English noblemen set off on "grand tours" to the Continent. Their mission was cultural enrichment and, though less widely advertised, carnal adventure. After graduation from Oxford or Cambridge, the moneyed young men headed for France and Italy on a voyage that was part self-discovery and part society debut, as they hobnobbed with their Continental counterparts and communed with the marvels of the Renaissance and classical civilization.

The grand tour was a crash course for the fortunate sons of the aristocracy (and, later, the upper-middle class) in the glittering triumphs of Western civilization. For young, upper-middle-class North Americans and Europeans, this kind of travel is reasonably familiar. The grand tour is essentially a more imaginative name for the study abroad experience, or the "gap year" trip more common among other Anglos and Europeans. This was, of course, a more rarefied trip than today's semester in Florence and a three-month Eurail pass. The grand tourists trekked to view great art (the only way to see a Michelangelo in those days was in person, since photography did not exist yet), to polish up their language skills (this was the same pool from which the diplomatic corps would be drawn), and to meet spirited women or other men (or simply to rent them). They set out with a retinue of servants, had portraits painted, and generally ambled and shambled their way through the salons and streets of Europe.

Italy was the summit for the grand tourists. The fetish for Italian history and sensuality, in food or art or romance, is definitely nothing new. Rome was the antithesis of London. As the epicenter of Catholicism, it was the seat of a great geopolitical rival. In the aftermath of the Reformation, the Catholic pilgrimage that Erasmus would ridicule was replaced by the grand tour, a worshipful encounter with the patrimony of Western art and civilization of antiquity. The same journey, from England to Rome, that had impelled English pilgrims in medieval times was repurposed for contemporary sensibilities—as if the journey's attraction actually preceded any particular religious or spiritual basis. The voyage was the constant, and the rationale changed with time.

If Rome had lost its religious attraction, it still represented a pinnacle of culture. In a sense, this was the point. Culture was the fence that the nobility built around itself to enforce its own social status. By immersing itself in cultures that only the well resourced could pursue, it could build the fence even higher—and require a boat to reach it. One result was a noble class in England that felt more intimately connected to continental life and culture than to the rest of British society. This wasn't a uniquely British problem, or a new one. In Russia, the elite of Saint Petersburg were similarly pulling away from Russian culture; privileged children grew up in the French language, engrossed in Francophilia, exposed to ordinary Russians only through servants and nursemaids. Whereas the Petersburg elite imported a French lifestyle and affect to their own country, the English carved out some time in postadolescence for a diverting trip.

The diversion part of the equation was important, too. These expeditions brought young men into a more permissive milieu ("What happens in Rome, stays in Rome"). The tour was an outlet for impulses that were inconvenient at home, such as extramarital and same-sex affairs. For the young and very fortunate, there was a thrill to transgressing these confessional, imperial, and moral boundaries. Ultimately, though, it was an offense that only reinforced their rank.

The effects of the grand tour on British culture were far reaching. Travel literature, which flourished during the period, as so many educated and cultivated young men were heading abroad, was the primary channel for education about fine art. Most Britons were only dimly aware of the Renaissance; the writings of grand tourists brought its riches into the national consciousness. The English country house—an emblem of the age—came into style as travelers needed space to display their artifacts and souvenirs from their trips. Like the scallop shells gathered by pilgrims on the Camino de Santiago to declare their status as sacred travelers, and to carry home as social verification, the collection of artifacts for display at home became an important legacy of the grand tour, for the travelers and for British high society at large. Of course, gathering a few shells is a far sight from traveling with an official portraitist, as some English did. Italian artists also saw profit in catering to British visitors. Besides portraits of vacationing aristocrats, some Italian artists made handsome livings copying Old Masters paintings on commission, presumably for the walls of English country homes and the like.

Though the experience was broadening, in many respects, it also reinforced the chauvinisms of the English abroad. While the grandeur of the ancient empires was profound, the travelers were also keenly aware of just how far once-great civilizations had declined. The historian Edward Gibbon, already an intellectual of some note when he set off on his grand tour, was inspired by the ancient ruins to begin his classic work, *The Decline and Fall of the Roman Empire*. Gibbon wrote in his memoirs:

> It was at Rome, on the fifteenth of October 1764, as I sat musing amidst the ruins of the Capitol, while the barefooted fryars were singing Vespers in the temple of Jupiter, that the idea of writing the decline and fall of the City first started to my mind.

Like many tourists, the English in Europe found their travels to be affably exotic, enriching but ultimately unthreatening to their sense of order.

The French Revolution disrupted access to the continent, and the grand tours were largely suspended. After the revolution, the British elite returned to Paris and Rome. But by that time, the age of mass tourism had begun. The grand tourists documented their frustration. Lord Byron wrote in a letter from Venice dated March 25, 1817:

> I wished to have gone to Rome, but at present it is pestilent with English—a parcel of staring boobies, who go about gaping and wishing to be at once cheap and magnificent.

Almost as soon as tourism began as a mass enterprise, there was a backlash among those who wished to distinguish themselves from the sordid crowds. Wealthy travelers felt some propriety toward the continental capitals and they didn't like sharing the cobbled squares with middle-class sightseers. They started looking for destinations farther afield, like the Balkans and Middle East. In other words, nearly as soon as modern tourism begins, we already see a kind of class anxiety that seeks to separate the tourist from the "real traveler." Often the distinction came down to those with the resources to go alone, in contrast to those who traveled in more economical groups. The historian Jeremy Black states in a podcast recorded for the National Gallery in London in March 2008:

> In many senses, tourism in the eighteenth century is much more interesting than tourism today because it is a much more individual art. You might well have at any one time no more than twenty prominent aristocrats and maybe another sixty British travelers for pleasure in Italy at the time, so it's not like going on a package holiday or anything—this is very much individual tourism. These are individuals who when they go to Italy follow in many senses their own individualized response to the landscape, to the activities that they can do.

A few important changes were happening in the years after the end of the Napoleonic Wars in 1815. Railways were being built across the Continent that made travel easier and cheaper; tourism was a way for rail companies to maximize their investments in infrastructure. A growing middle class was looking to share in the travel experience, both as a public demonstration of their upward mobility and as a rite of induction into the world of the cultured elite. By midcentury, 165,000 vacationers crossed the English Channel. By century's end, it was nearly a million.

Frances Trollope, a keen satirist of the English and a gifted travel writer herself, published her sardonic novel *The Robertses on Their Travels* in 1846. Already a sensation after publishing her travelogue *Domestic Manners of the Americans*, in which she skewered Americans as crude, hypocritical, and self-involved, Mrs. Trollope (as she was known to her fans) lampooned fellow Englishmen who aspired to Continental sophistication. The Robertses were ambitious middle-class Londoners who hoped to raise their social status by decamping to Europe. A year on the Continent, they believed, would be both cost effective and socially uplifting. Mrs. Roberts insists that her son Edward leave Oxford immediately to join them; he had already learned all the Greek and Latin he would need to become a schoolmaster. Mrs. Roberts insists:

> Modern languages, Mr Roberts, must now be added to the accomplishments for which he is already so remarkable. Modern languages and waltzing will render him as nearly perfect as it is within the reach of human nature to be.

The first grand tourists, scions of the gentry, looked to raise their status by consuming the culture of Europe. The Robertses wanted access to Europe in order to be more like the gentry.

If there is an inventor of modern tourism, it must be Thomas Cook; he thought up nothing less than the idea of the round-trip ticket. He was prescient about many things. His business invented or consolidated much of what we now know as the modern tourism industry. Recognizing and harnessing the power of the railway to move people cheaply and comfortably was a key to Cook's eventual success. The scope of that success was astonishing.

The company had its own specialty newspaper, called the *Excursionist*, which sold ads for Paris hotels. They sold vacations with fixed itineraries and all-inclusive entertainment. They helped English-speaking tourists maneuver in French. Cook was part ringmaster, concierge, valet, and Sherpa. In 1866, he shipped the first European tourists off to the New World.

Cook was a passionate advocate of temperance, and in 1841 he organized a dry train journey to spread the good word. Temperance supporters believed that alcohol was the root of social ills in Victorian England. He was an idealist and an evangelist. In 1845, he began to explore the commercial potential of organized popular tourism. The next year, he began organizing trips to Scotland, which gave many English their first exposure to the Scottish Highlands. In the 1850s, he made his first visit to the Continent, to the Paris Exhibition. Over the next decade, he took groups to Switzerland, America, and Egypt. In 1872, he organized his first round-the-world trip, lasting 222 days.

It was his son, John Mason Cook, who recognized the potential for a mass tourism industry, with their company at the forefront. The first goal for the junior Cook was to raise the cachet of the company, and the potential revenue, by appealing to wealthier travelers. To bring in those who would not be enticed by cheap fares only, the company began to offer premium services that were essentially new, like rail timetables, guidebooks, travelers' checks, and uniformed valets. By the 1880s, Thomas Cook and Sons was transporting British troops up the Nile. The Indian government enlisted the company to help ferry pilgrims to Mecca. They were the official travel partners of the first modern Olympic Games. They even organized a private tour of the Holy Land for the German kaiser. A company slogan from the 1920s: "From the heir to the throne to the humblest greengrocer, they all travel with Thomas Cook."

Tourists can be a vexing presence, and not only for the privileged travelers who seem to think that the presence of tourists undermines the importance of their own journeys. Tourism and the industry that supports it leave a mark on a place, influencing economics, politics, culture, and the environment. There are psychic tolls, too, more difficult to quantify but often powerfully felt. The Antiguan author Jamaica Kincaid wrote a short, scathing book called *A Small Place* (1988), about returning to her tiny Caribbean island after years abroad. She came to the United States at seventeen to work as an au pair. Because of conflicts with her family, she largely cut herself off from the island culture, even changing her name so that people back home wouldn't know she was writing. In the novel, when she finally returns for a visit, she experiences many kinds of turmoil. Some arise from the inevitable dislocation of returning to a once-familiar place to find that it has not stayed just as you remember. There is the melancholy feeling of being unaccustomed to a place that is in some deep respect still your home; this can be a painful affront to our sense of self, since identity and place have a deep codependency.

But the changes she observes are, by no means, purely a matter of inner psychology. Antigua has changed in tangible ways, in many ways that bring Kincaid real despair. Her ire and frustration are directed, with critical fury and cutting wit, at the tourists who have made a playground of her island. The tourists are plunderers. They come to take what is beautiful and exotic and cheap and leave behind only scraps and waste. Much of the book is written as a one-sided argument with a faceless but emblematic tourist. Her judgment is swift and damning:

> The thing you always suspected about yourself the minute you became a tourist is true: A tourist is an ugly human being. You are not an ugly person all the time; you are not an ugly person ordinarily; you are not an ugly person day to day. From day to day, you are a nice person. From day to day, all the people who are supposed to love you on the whole do.

What makes an ugly tourist out of a nice person? Kincaid refuses to let the tourist stand apart from her historical context, from the relationships of power and inequality that underlie the whole arrangement. In short, good people become ugly tourists when they mistake personal virtue, or simple good behavior, for conscientious travel. Tourists are for Kincaid another manifestation of colonial imposition, which takes everything worth having and—though it promises civility and prosperity—leaves only ill will and bad faith and a poor excuse for a civil society. Kincaid demands:

> Have you ever wondered why all people like me seem to have learned from you is how to imprison and murder each other, how to govern badly, and how to take the wealth of our country and place it in a Swiss bank account?

Kincaid thinks the solution is relatively straightforward: "Don't come," she says. Lord Byron would probably agree, at least for the middle-class tourists that he found so distracting.

SO FAR, WE HAVE talked about travel as an enduring human enterprise. Travel is embedded in the origins of species, in our journey from the African plains to every other corner of the inhabited world. It is central to our mythology and our earliest efforts to comprehend the human condition and make sense of the world around us. These are important insights but they should not blind us to the fact that travel has changed enormously through the ages, and the rate of change has accelerated to an almost dizzying degree in recent generations. In fact, we now have to entertain possible futures that are both incongruous and alarming. The changes have come so fast and furiously that we must contemplate some drastic scenarios that would have been unimaginable not long ago. We can imagine travel beyond the limits of our own world. At the same time, we are obliged to reckon with the possibility of a world without travel.

The incredible mobility of people, capital, and ideas that gave us Western modernity did not come from nowhere. Though we have discussed many of the important ideas and discoveries that led to the age of mass movement, there is another critical ingredient without which none of this could have happened. From its discovery in the 1850s, oil has been the engine of our progress, accelerating growth to a previously unimaginable velocity. From 1900 to the present, humans have consumed more energy than in all previous human history. Ninety-five percent of all manufactured goods, and a similar percentage of all of our food, depend on oil for production.

The means of travel often become metaphors of progress. Think of how trains are depicted in movies: as conduits of economic transformation. In *Walden*, Henry David Thoreau said, "We do not ride on the railroad; it rides upon us."

The technologies that enable our mobility are just as intertwined with fossil fuels and the oil economy. The twentieth century began with the arrival of oil-burning automobiles and aviation. The social transformations and political experiments of the century—unprecedented in human history—have a crucial debt to these innovations. Certainly there would be no American Century without the automobile and the airplane. American preeminence in culture, industry, and military power was only possible because of its vast consumption and its geopolitical grasp on the world oil supply.

In 1972, W. H. Auden wrote his poem "A Curse," about the havoc wrought by fossil fuels. Auden would die the following year, during the OPEC oil embargo, one of the first modern moments when the anxiety of scarcity entered the mainstream consciousness. Auden writes:

Dark was that day when Diesel
conceived his grim engine that
begot you, vile invention

Auden could see, at the end of his life, the helplessness of our fuel dependence. He understood that oil was the foundation for the fictions we told ourselves about our world and where it was headed.

Our seemingly boundless growth was predicated on a pre-sumed-to-be-boundless supply of oil. The unspoken assumption that our resources were infinite led many to believe that human potential itself was infinite. The ease with which we were able to cross borders and continents stoked the belief that all borders and all obstacles were surmountable. We felt ourselves to be on a trajectory toward total control of the environment. We could go as fast as we wanted, grow and consume whatever we needed, and make our surroundings conform to our specifications. In this way, of course, the hubris and stupor induced by oil is perfectly embodied in the modern tourist. Modern tourism is built on the same myth of abundance.

The cruise ship, in fact, might be the perfect symbol of the late capitalist fever dream. Cruise ships and their passengers are often maligned; for various reasons, some to do with class and aesthetics and others with ecology and social impact, cruises are often seen as the nadir of bourgeois travel.

Condescension aside, there is justification for this. In 2013, the cruise industry earned more than its usual share of bad press. A lifeboat accident killed five crewmembers of a Thomson cruise ship. A fire on a Carnival cruise ship nearly stranded three thousand people in the Gulf of Mexico. According to a report in the *Daily Mail*:

> By Tuesday night, passengers were sending messages about the stench from feces and urine and dwindling food supplies. Mattresses had been hauled to hallways and the deck where sleeping was a bit cooler. Tension and fear were running high. On Thursday, Julie Hair called her husband from the ship to report that their 12-year-old daughter had Skittles candy for breakfast and that she ate cold waffles. The smell on board "was horrendous," she said. "We thought the toilet was flushing today, but the water was coming up."

In January 2012, the Italian *Costa Concordia*—a vessel the length of two football fields, weighing sixty thousand tons—ran aground on a coastal reef and thirty-two passengers drowned. The captain was allegedly attempting a daredevil maneuver with the 4,200-passenger ship, and then abandoned the ship by raft as it sank. The ship lay on its side in the harbor for nearly two years before salvage began. Cleanup is still under way. The total cost is likely to be around $1 billion.

And these are just the most spectacular incidents. The routine mayhem of the cruise industry is far more devastating. Ship operators have been fined repeatedly for pollution, often through willful criminal behavior. In 1999, Royal Caribbean International pleaded guilty to twenty-one counts of dumping oil and hazardous chemicals and deceiving the U.S. Coast Guard. They agreed to pay $18 million. The next year, the company was fined $3.5 million for dumping toxic chemicals and contaminated water into the ocean near Alaska. In 2013, the Cruise Report Card from the organization Friends of the Earth gave very low marks to most cruise lines in sewage treatment, air pollution reduction, and water quality. The cruise industry continues to fight efforts to regulate its environmental impact and has advocated for voluntary self-monitoring.

The cruise lines expend all kinds of energy on controlling and managing the environment aboard the ships. A similar effort is made on shore, to carefully choreograph the passengers' interaction with their destinations. For the most part, the motivations are easy enough to see: their interest is in creating a safe, predictable experience that encourages tourists to spend money on businesses who pay back commissions to the ship lines. But offering surprise-free shopping jaunts to poor, fragile countries is a massive undertaking. It has led operators to construct elaborate archipelagos of tourist insularity, Potemkin villages for paying customers only.

To take one extreme—but not isolated—example: three days after a massive earthquake shook Haiti in 2010, the Royal Caribbean company resumed dockings in Labadee, their customary port. Labadee is a private beach, leased by Royal Caribbean from the Haitian government. The company has invested $50 million in the site, making it the largest foreign investor in Haiti. Labadee is just sixty miles from the epicenter of the quake, which claimed as many as 200,000, though it was unaffected. It is also a self-contained economy. Though the site employs some three hundred locals in mostly low-wage jobs, Royal Caribbean kept the circle of beneficiaries quite small. A large wall, guarded by private security, encircles the tourist area. This is the kind of superficial contact with destinations that typifies cruise experiences. Though there are certainly exceptions, most cruise ships average just ten hours per port, and dockings typically happen in heavily curated environments like Labadee.

Within a few days of the earthquake, as many as fifteen thousand tourists docked. About 120 pallets of food were donated to relief efforts. For a weeklong trip, a large cruise ship will typically load up with at least 750 pallets.

The cruise ships would probably prefer that passengers not think about life on the other side of that wall. They'd rather you weren't thinking of Haiti at all. On board the ship, the destination is marked as "Labadee, Hispaniola," the name given to the island by Christopher Columbus. A Royal Caribbean manager told the *Christian Science Monitor* in an interview, "The real question is 'Where is Haiti?'—and 'What is Haiti?' If you are honest, even if you tell them, most passengers don't know where they are, usually."

Whatever might lie ahead, tourism is for now only expanding in the new century. What was once an industry that catered primarily to the wealthier segments of the Northern Hemisphere is quickly becoming a truly global phenomenon.

By far, the most significant new players are the Chinese people and the Chinese government. Chinese tourists are now the top spenders globally. In 2012, Chinese citizens took some 83 million foreign trips and spent about $100 billion abroad. Most believe this is just a foretaste of what is to come. According to the World Tourism Organization, in less than ten years Chinese tourists are projected to make 200 million trips abroad, making them the dominant force in global tourism by a substantial margin. And the world is getting ready. In Paris, the most coveted destination among Chinese, a variety of civic forces are working diligently to make the city friendlier to the growing hordes. From Chinese-speaking hotel staff to Chinese food, the French are rolling out the hospitality on a scale not seen since the boom in postwar American tourism.

This is an astonishing shift, not just for tourist destinations around the world but also for the Chinese themselves. Before 1978, when the government began to gradually initiate economic reforms, travel was beyond the experience or aspirations of all but the most privileged and connected Chinese. Besides political restrictions, endemic poverty put travel out of reach for the great majority.

As part of measures to boost local consumer markets, restrictions on mobility were eased over time and the state began to encourage domestic travel in the 1980s. Today, the Chinese domestic tourism market is enormous, with as many as 1.7 billion domestic tourist trips each year. The hospitality industry employs about 10 percent of all Chinese workers, some 80 million people.

For those looking to conjure a Chinese tourism industry into existence, practically by fiat, economic reforms were only a piece of the puzzle. To really generate a thriving tourism industry, far-reaching cultural changes were also necessary. In 1995, the government established the five-day work week. The next year, 1996, was declared the Year of Leisure and Vacation.

The Chinese had to create the concept of leisure travel in their modernization effort to capitalize on tourism. Accompanying such policy changes were the growth of *xiuxian wenhua* (the culture of leisure) and *luyou wenhua* (the culture of travel), as well as the creation of a leisure industry to support the new demand. *Luyou re* (the craze for travel) is a neologism for an invented notion.

Like the Americans before them, the Chinese are already getting a bad reputation as boorish and undesirable guests. The problem has become so acute that China's National Tourism Administration has published a brochure titled, roughly, "Guide to Civilized Tourism and Travel." Tips include theater etiquette ("If the performer makes a mistake, you must forgive him and not heckle, whistle, or boo him") and hotel pool use ("Don't spit in a hotel pool—and absolutely never urinate in one"). A particularly ominous entry advises, "Don't take a long time using public toilets" and "Don't leave footprints on the toilet seat."

The hunger for tourism dollars and attention makes strange bedfellows. A report from Japan describes the country's efforts to appeal to Muslim travelers. A halal-certified udon noodle shop is now open in Kansai International Airport. Future plans at the airport include prayer rooms, and many restaurants on the premises won't serve alcohol or pork. The report continues:

> Japan is not alone in courting Southeast Asia's burgeoning middle class. Thailand has touted its halal spas, while hospitals in South Korea are building prayer rooms for those in town for a nip and tuck. New Zealand is going after Islamic foodies with a culinary tourism guide for halal travelers, and anticipates that spending by Muslim tourists will increase to more than 13% of global tourism expenditure by 2020.

Changes in global tourism are dramatically impacting even time-honored traditions. In Saudi Arabia, some 3 million Muslims descend annually for the Hajj pilgrimage. The Koran commands all able Muslims to make the trip at least once in their lives. While the Hajj is strongly associated with the prophet Muhammad, some rituals are believed to stretch back as far as the time of Abraham. The itinerary is carefully choreographed and highly prescribed. Millions of pilgrims gather to circle around the Kaaba, a black cube at the very center of the Grand Mosque of Mecca. It is one of humanity's great spectacles. They travel to Mount Ararat, the site of the prophet's last sermon. They enact a ritual stoning of the devil, each pilgrim gathering forty-nine rocks. Animals are sacrificed, heads are shaved. The pilgrims return to Mecca, performing a final circuit around the Kaaba.

As populations surge and travel becomes cheaper and easier, officials project that as many as 17 million pilgrims will visit Mecca and Medina by 2025. Crowds have grown and stampede deaths have become a grim reality of the event. Thousands have died in the last two decades. Saudi Arabia has started to limit the number of visas offered to foreign pilgrims—a deeply consequential barrier to a practice that is one of the five pillars of Islam. The backlog and waiting lists are growing around the world, with some waiting years for the chance to make the trip. In some countries, demand is so high that hajj experiences are being offered virtually, via video.

With greater crowds have also come opportunities for big business. Pilgrims have religious motivations for their travel, but they have many of the same needs as other tourists. Hajj is a global industry. A major trade event in London, the World Hajj and Umrah Convention, is, according to their website, "attended by over 200 delegates, government ministers, corporate representatives, key advisory groups and Hajj service providers." The Saudi tourism ministry reports revenues of more than $17 billion. A fast rail link between Mecca and Medina, costing some $6 billion, is in the works. The Grand Mosque is now surrounded by towering hotels and skyscrapers. Mountains have been razed and traditional neighborhoods have been leveled to make room for luxury developments and big-ticket entertainment. The Abraj Al Bait hotel complex now dominates the vista. One of the tallest buildings in the world, it is crowned with a clock tower that vaguely resembles Big Ben but is even more festooned. It is pure architectural pastiche, artlessly blending various Eastern and Western clichés. It dwarfs the mosque and can be seen from twenty miles away. The tourist gold rush has created a real estate bubble of astounding proportions, even by the global standards of the twenty-first century. A square foot of real estate in Manhattan now averages about $1,100, which is hardly a bargain. Prime properties around the Grand Mosque now sell for $18,000 per square foot.

In 2014, another bit of modernity encroached on the traditional proceedings. An entrepreneur in Dubai (a Lebanese American) created a mobile app to cater to pilgrims, called Hajj Salam. The app, which, by midyear, was downloaded more than forty thousand times, counts your circles around the Kaaba (using GPS). It gives easy-to-follow instructions for complicated rituals, with instructional videos and pronunciation guides for non-Arabic speakers. It can help you find hotels and ATMs. It also allows you to write social media status updates, keep checklists, and share photos with your friends online.

The dilemma of expanding global tourism is also the paradox of the world of growing prosperity. Parts of the world previously mired in poverty have seen fortunes rise and opportunities increase. After watching the high-consumption lifestyles of richer nations from afar for generations, another billion or so humans are ready to get in on the action. It's hard to begrudge them, even as awareness of the costs of such indulgence is growing in the West, some two hundred years after the Industrial Revolution.

Travel may be exciting, but it has consequences—not only for us, but for the places we visit. Our arrival disquiets them. The landscape and culture are changed by our presence. The idea of a pure, untouched environment and of a static culture is Romantic. The Romantics (Lord Byron, Goethe, José Martí) viewed Nature as their temple. But they didn't contemplate the transformation of Nature as a result of their presence. Instead, they thought Nature was permanent. Unfortunately, we know better. The rapid growth of human society has a deep impact on the planet. Fewer places remain pristine, unaffected by our restless, ceaseless movement.

A new age of tourism, if not exploration, may also be here. The era that saw the end of NASA space travel is also the era of the space-travel entrepreneur. The owner of the world's biggest store, Jeff Bezos of Amazon, is spending considerable time and resources realizing the possibility of commercial space travel for leisure. For the superwealthy and hyperambitious, space is truly the final frontier. Space is the place into which we can project all of our dissatisfactions with earthly existence, with the limits of our mortal power. The *Guardian* writes of Bezos:

> His long-term plan has always been something even grander: to establish a permanent human colony in space. His mother still has a copy of a speech he made at school declaring his

ambition to build a fleet of habitable orbiting space stations and turn the planet into a vast nature reserve.

How different is our view of space from that of explorers and travelers of the past? In many ways, the planets of our solar system seem less conceptually distant than the mythical East might have seemed to Marco Polo. Countless explorers in the past believed they had reached the "final frontier"—the outer limit of travel, somewhere beyond imagination—and many more regarded foreigners as essentially alien. From an environmental, political, and humanitarian point of view, the full implications of commercial, recreational space travel are staggering to ponder.

The future of travel is uncertain. We might be at the end of the great age of mobility, or we might be entering an era of leisure unprecedented in human history. This could be tourism's extravagant dying gasp, or we could just be gathering steam toward a world of perpetual motion. Given the profound changes that seem to be ahead of us, it might be an opportune time to rethink the underlying values and assumptions of this peculiar human enterprise. It's time for a new ethics of travel.

7

TRAVELING OUTSIDE
THE FRAME

The age of photography has been coincident with the age of mass travel. Or perhaps we should say simultaneous, because there is nothing coincidental about it: photography helped create an appetite for tourism. In the mid-nineteenth century, alluring glimpses of strange places came to the Western public in the form of photographs. Landscapes and architectural images, often muted and hazy—photography in its early period was technically primitive—had the exotic magnetism of Xanadu.

The English scientist William Henry Fox Talbot was a traveler and frustrated painter. His main interests—art, science, and anthropology—converged in the nascent practice of photography. On a trip to Italy, the story goes, Fox Talbot was sitting by a magnificent lake with a palette and easel, despairing over his sheer inability to paint the scene realistically or beautifully. A few years later, Fox Talbot presented his "art of photogenic drawing" to the Royal Society. He would soon patent a photographic process that put him in competition with the more-famous Daguerre. He has a legitimate, if certainly not sole, claim to the title "inventor" of photography as we know it (unlike the daguerreotype, which reproduced an image directly onto a copper plate, Fox Talbot's calotype printed from a negative onto paper, so multiple copies could be made). He was inarguably the first to publish a book with photo illustrations. The book's title tells us how Fox Talbot felt about the new medium's potential: he called it *The Pencil of Nature*.

By the 1850s, not long after Fox Talbot began publishing photographs from the boulevards of Paris, and as contemporaries made images of the Acropolis, Thebes, Burma, the Alps, and other remote locations, Thomas Cook began offering inexpensive group trips to Paris.

With the explosion of modern photography—which is to say, portable photography—motion became the paramount aesthetic value of twentieth-century art, just as it became a signifier of social refinement for the upwardly mobile. Technology liberated photography from the stationary around the same time new transit technologies were giving unprecedented freedom of movement to middle-class Westerners.

Shortly before World War I, an obscure German optical engineer and mechanic named Oskar Barnack developed the first camera designed to shoot 35 mm film (the format became the standard from photojournalism to family snapshots until the digital age). Why did it matter? Barnack was an asthmatic, and lugging around the heavy equipment of the day was a burden. With 35 mm film, the camera became smaller and lighter. Just as important, the film was faster. You could capture sharp images with fast shutter speeds; in other words, you could hold the camera in your hands, without a tripod. The photographer Robert Capa brought a camera of Barnack's design along to the battlefields of the Spanish Civil War. He captured images unlike any the world had seen: the photographer was now right at the center of the action, on location, arresting crucial moments, splicing seconds into discrete artifacts.

For the masters of this modern approach to photography—great names like André Kertész, Henri Cartier-Bresson, Robert Frank—movement became the real subject of photography. The ephemerality of a scene was integral to its beauty and meaning.

Cartier-Bresson called it "the decisive moment"—certainly photography's most famous dictum, and still its most incisive. In fact, the term was not exactly Cartier-Bresson's own. He was borrowing the phrase from Cardinal de Retz in the seventeenth century: "Il n'y a rien dans ce monde qui n'ait un moment decisive." This was for the preface to a book titled *Images à la Sauvette*, which is more closely translated as *Image on the Run* or *Furtive Images*. His American publisher chose *The Decisive Moment*. None of these choices seem exactly inapt, but the different shades of meaning conveyed are significant and revealing.

The French title makes the process of image making seem frenetic, aleatory, even illicit. The English version has a judicious and patient feel; the photographer is in control of the situation, making critical decisions on the fly, a sure-eyed arbiter who can separate the durable reality from the randomness of an unfolding scene. Which association rings more true for you, as a viewer, has a real influence on how you understand the work in front of you.

Cartier-Bresson's 1932 *Behind the Saint-Lazare Train Station*, which unceremoniously captures a man jumping over a puddle, is probably the photographer's most famous frame. The figure, in silhouette, is in the air, legs splayed, his leading toe about to touch the ground. He is leaning forward, toward the edge of the frame. In the puddle's reflection, the figure is duplicated and inverted. The composition is both artless and absolutely perfect (he cropped the negative for the famous print, something he rarely did, and a practice he claimed to detest—he pledged fidelity to what the viewfinder saw and the film recorded). The frame is full of symmetry and visual rhyme. In the background, there is a poster with a stick-figure ballerina, legs also splayed, leaping in the opposite direction.

This is the decisive moment par excellence. And Cartier-Bresson is either extremely lucky or uncommonly gifted in his fleet-fingered perception. Both are possible, which is something you couldn't say of Ansel Adams or Edward Weston. Those photographers were obsessive arrangers, fine-tuners, and autocrats. Cartier-Bresson didn't enjoy the same control over his subject matter; Peter Pollack quotes him thus in his book *The Picture History of Photography*: "To me, photography is the simultaneous recognition, in a fraction of a second, of the significance of an event as well as of a precise organization of forms which give that event its proper expression."

From the early 1930s, with his first trip to Africa, Cartier-Bresson worked his way around the world. A relentless traveler, he was a progenitor of what we would now recognize as photojournalism. His career flourished alongside popular magazines such as *Life*. His work exemplifies some of the genre's best and worst traits. He cultivated an exquisitely sharp eye for local detail and a fascination with tradition and change. At the same time, there was something cold in his approach; his intuitions were far more aesthetic than humane. Although he was present for many moments of world-historic significance, and captured scenes of great human intensity, his work doesn't project the compassion of greater documentarians like Walker Evans or Dorothea Lange. He was a perfect twentieth-century update to Baudelaire's flaneur, an insightful but detached observer. The job requires certain risks and sensitivities, but it is generally a low-stakes bet when it comes to emotional engagement.

Robert Frank was severe—and probably right—in his critique of Cartier-Bresson's work. In an interview in 1975, Frank said: "He traveled all over the goddamned world, and you never felt that he was moved by something that was happening other than the beauty of it, or just the composition." Maybe he simply moved too fast. He covered too much ground. Cartier-Bresson's talent was to see acutely, rather than compassionately, and respond quickly. He was more interested in moving through places than arriving at them. His best photographs aren't about people; they are about the split-second geometries of bodies moving through space. His real subject was time, which happens everywhere.

The relationship between travel and photography has always leaned heavily on the medium's evidentiary claims: this photograph is proof of where I've been or what I've seen. Travel photographs are a kind of trophy, a less bloody version of the buck's head over the mantle.

PHOTOGRAPHY HAS ALWAYS had a tortured relationship to the truth. Robert Capa's *Death of a Loyalist Militiaman*, a photo of a soldier falling as he is pierced by a bullet, is certainly one of the most famous war images ever captured. Of the Capa photo, the critic Geoff Dyer, in a review in *Time* magazine of an exhibit called "War/Photography" at the Museum of Fine Arts in Houston, writes, "While photography is generally assumed to be strong as evidence but weak in meaning, Capa's photograph has come to resemble painting, of which the contrary is held to be true." Debates have raged for years over whether the photo was staged. The matter has been "indisputably" settled a dozen times or more.

These sorts of forensic studies have become a popular, if slightly perverse, habit of photography scholars. The question of veracity is certainly interesting and sometimes valuable. The *New York Times* published an illuminating article about the sleights-of-hand of the Russian American photographer Roman Vishniac. His iconic images of Eastern European Jews are not fakes, per se, but they take great liberties with context. Vishniac's sins are mostly, but not exclusively, of omission: the world he portrays is much less complex than the one he actually encountered on his travels. The Jewish ghettos he entered were more diverse, secular, and dynamic than his photographs would suggest. He focused selectively on a certain character typology he thought would resonate with his audience, in this case by affirming stereotypes of wan, defenseless, and pious Jews. He was trying, as they say, to paint a picture. As evidence, the photos are deficient. As polemic, they are effective.

Today, the evidentiary claim of photography has been substantially weakened, and we are rarely shocked to learn that photos have been manipulated or prejudicially edited. We have learned to doubt our own eyes, whether we are being shown military reconnaissance or a too-slender model.

Some contemporary photographers have taken up these questions in an enriching way. The Mexican photographer Pedro Meyer, who started out as a war correspondent in Nicaragua, has spent much of the digital photography era creating inscrutable images that are simply impossible to evaluate as representations of truth. He often uses the vernacular of black-and-white photojournalism to heighten the disorienting effect of an implausible image. The works can be seen as satire, novelty, surrealism, or all of the above. But, in any case, truth is beside the point.

Unsurprisingly, war photography—now an aesthetic tradition unto itself—is especially fertile ground for photographers who want to subvert the presumed realism of images. Simon Reynolds, a Briton who roams the world with a wood-and-brass field camera the size of a phone booth, has taken up both the journalistic and landscape traditions that hold travel and photography together. His series on mass-grave sites in Bosnia are both nature studies and forensic exhibits. Irish photojournalist Richard Mosse, who has covered the civil war in Congo, has created a striking book of infrared images that amplify reality with psychedelic colors.

"Photojournalists tend to avoid the dilemma of ethics and aesthetics—the problems that arise when you make aesthetic images from human suffering," Mosse said in an interview with journalist Laura Davis. "Very few people consider any alternatives to the Capa low-fi, grainy, black-and-white approach." His photographs also remind us how banal even the most nightmarish images have become, simply because we encounter them so often. These pictures are harder to ignore than typical news stills. The flamboyant aesthetic doesn't minimize the subjects' pain—something any decent-minded photojournalist must contemplate. Mosse's distorted palette—electric pink, restored browns, blood crimson—are like the pressure gauges on the artist's emotional and moral outrage.

In the age of Google Maps, travel photography may not even require travel. Here, the most basic evidentiary claim is undermined. When American photographer Michael Wolf moved to Paris for his wife's job, he was uninterested in exploring the city of Cartier-Bresson in the conventional way. Instead, he sits at his computer in his home office and cruises the streets virtually on Google, looking for serendipitous moments of photographic interest. He finds ample material: an old woman crumpled on the curb, a kissing couple, a nude swimmer. The work feels uniquely contemporary, but one wonders if he shouldn't have taken it further. He has selected frames from the infinite record of the Google satellite feed, but he mostly replicates the vantage of a photographer standing a few feet away on a crowded street, as he would with a 35 mm Leica. Is that what should define an interesting image amid this deluge of information? It's a neat demonstration, but it's a stylistic cul-de-sac.

Far more interesting than anything happening in the professional realm of photography are the enormous changes in how photography functions in daily life. Picture taking is more popular than ever, even as we are learning to doubt some of its first principles. Estimates suggest that humans are collectively producing as many as 1.2 billion images per day, which is about half a trillion images each year. Even if we can't trust the veracity of images after Photoshop, the sheer ubiquity of photography allows it to make other claims to reliability.

To test this hypothesis, ask yourself the following question: Can you imagine a significant public event that isn't documented in some way by its participants? If you heard news of a major incident on a Manhattan street at 5 PM, would you be a little skeptical if no video turned up on YouTube? You probably should.

THERE IS PROBABLY a camera in your pocket right now. Maybe it's on the table next to you. But it's a safe bet that you could pick up a camera right now without leaving your chair. This fact is an extraordinary change and challenge to photography, and it has profound implications for how we travel and go about our daily lives.

In the age of mobile phones and pocket cameras, photography has gone from being a by-product of travel to a raison d'être. Visit any popular destination and you'll likely find more people staring at three-inch LCD screens than looking directly at any particular attraction. First we document, then we experience.

We are shown travel photographs as if they were trophies. The traveler near the Pyramids, exploring the Mayan ruins in Yucatán, on a bicycle in Beijing. The photo says it all: the voyage was done in order for the image to be taken. The face in the photo has a forced, plastic smile. "Look at me doing this!" it says. This image is proof of how far I have gone, the place I have visited. As Susan Sontag put it in her meditation *On Photography*, "Travel becomes a strategy for accumulating photographs."

It seems as if there is a crisis of experience going on, or maybe it's a pervasive anxiety about our powers of recall and perception. If only photographs matter, then we can't afford not to have a camera near us. Telephone companies have solved our dilemma: include a camera in your iPhone. Use it everywhere you go: in the classroom, at parties, in marches. And share it with others because an unshared photograph is like an unread letter. When others see it, its message blooms, it becomes effectual.

What does a photograph do? It freezes time. It makes a single moment eternal. And it does more: it forces on the world the perspective of an individual. Of course, that has always been the prerogative of art. But photography adds another quality: verisimilitude. Unlike a canvas, unlike a sculpture, unlike a play, it makes the viewer believe the universe is contained in the image. It isn't make-believe but the thing itself, it states. So why is photography an art? Because that idea of verisimilitude is bogus. The universe is still the universe. Nothing has changed in it. Or maybe something: now there is a mechanical re-creation of it.

No two individuals are alike. Likewise, unless they are actual copies, all photographs are different from one another. That's because the viewer changes, internally as well as externally. What he sees depends on his position: where he is exactly. Move him an inch and the perspective is different. For, as Heraclitus proved, no one enters the same river twice. The world moves and we move in it. Nothing is static, least of all one's viewpoint.

Photographs are endlessly malleable. The photographer toys with them, personalizing their content. What we see isn't Truth with capital T but truth: subjective, partial, replaceable. Still, photographs make us see things differently. Imagine a society without them. What would be different? The capacity to be self-conscious, the realization that we're always in control of our movement. Photographs make us simultaneously actors and witnesses. They force us to see the universe and be seen in it.

The British photographer Martin Parr is probably the greatest visual commentator on the relationship of photography to tourism; his work is obsessed with tourists and their distorting effect on people and landscapes. Parr observed in the essay "Too Much Photography":

> One thing that has really changed in recent years is how the tourist uses photography. When I started shooting this topic many years ago, people would take one photo of themselves in front of the site and move on. Now mobile phone cameras and digital photography mean that the entire visit is documented. From the moment the tourist enters the site, everyone has to be photographed in front of every feature of note. Now it is almost impossible for me to shoot a photo where someone is NOT taking a picture or posing for one.

The implications, for Parr, go well beyond the content of his own images or even the practice of photography. He worries, "The photographic record of the visit has almost destroyed the very notion of actually looking." This is probably too sweeping, but the irony is still unmistakable. In the past, photography conditioned us to be curious travelers. Now photography threatens to cut us off from the experiences we set out to record. The camera, with its omnipresence and its colossal reach, becomes the obstacle to engagement.

Or better, the camera becomes the one item we are always engaged with, to the point that the trip is really about our relationship with the photographs the camera produces. We doctor those images, we curate them. If we don't like the rays of the sun, we darken them. And is that chair not in the right position? Click: now it's no longer there. The world, as it is, is endlessly adaptable to our voyeuristic hunger. We don't really live in it. Instead, we live in order to reconfigure it.

Italo Calvino wrote a short story, long before the age of Instagram and social image sharing, called "The Adventure of a Photographer," making an argument that should give us pause today:

The line between the reality that is photographed because it seems beautiful to us and the reality that seems beautiful because it has been photographed is very narrow. . . . You only have to start saying of something: "Ah, how beautiful! We must photograph it!" and you are already close to the view of the person who thinks that everything that is not photographed is lost, as if it had never existed, and that therefore in order really to live you must photograph as much as you can, and to photograph as much as you can you must either live in the most photographable way possible, or else consider photographable every moment of your life. The first course leads to stupidity; the second, to madness.

This relationship between the reality that is photographed and the reality that is beautiful because it has been photographed— the relationship, according to Calvino, between stupidity and madness—is also explored, albeit from another perspective, by Michelangelo Antonioni's 1966 film *Blow-Up*. In it a fashion photographer is shooting images with a model in a park when a murder apparently takes place. His lens inadvertently captures the crime, although the photographer doesn't know it until he returns to his lab to develop the images. Yet, as those images roll out in front of him, he realizes it was the camera that might have prompted the murder to be committed. In other words, the witness to the crime is also—improbably—its cause.

That is because the presence of a camera adds a layer of subjectivity to events: what happens is now framed by what the lens says happens. In Antonioni's movie, this statement is taken to the next level as the filmmaker turns the lens into the narrator of the entire plot. Not the fashion designer's eye, which, after all, is commanded by its owner, but the camera itself, which is given a will of its own by the Italian director. This strategy makes sense. After all, one gets the impression today that life happens so it might be photographed.

There is another strange dimension to photography's populist turn: a nostalgic conceit that makes a fetish of old-fashioned vacation snaps. Popular photo-sharing platforms like Instagram and Hipstamatic have caught on wildly by making it easy to dress up smartphone images—which are certainly getting better all the time, but tend to be aesthetically bland—in the stylized, wistful look of much older photographs. They simulate the look of film from the 1960s, down-sample data to mimic plastic Soviet-era cameras, gratuitously add sprocket holes and borders to make it look like you pulled the image out of a shoebox from your grandmother's attic.

This is what photography teaches us about ourselves today: everything is important, but nothing is memorable. Sontag, again in *On Photography*, believed that "the camera makes everyone a tourist of other people's reality, and eventually of one's own." What is not photographed, and shared, is lost. Or never happened at all. How strange that we seem to have so little faith in our own capacity to remember—or even to recognize and authentically experience an event as it is happening, for ourselves. This seems like another symptom of the crisis of experience, an anxiety over our ability to leave a mark in a world of passing fancies and digital rot. This is what the critic Svetlana Boym, in *The Future of Nostalgia*, means by "the hypochondria of the heart." Nostalgia is a shortcut to significance; it is cheap insurance against forgetting.

8

THE INDUSTRY
OF FAKE EXPERIENCE

The more things change, the more we crave the same. The world appears to be spinning in new directions. Life has never been so complex. Humans have never before had to contend with so much new information, so much competition for attention, such speed and complexity, such interdependence with others. When everything seems both new and terrifying, our collective response has been to fabricate our own meaningful patterns, to create the illusion of familiarity.

We have twin desires: authenticity and oblivion. Authenticity speaks to our crises of confidence, our anxiety about the spiritual credibility of modern lives. Rousseau used the term "authenticity" to mean existence itself. It is our authentic nature, which society only degrades. Is that the same kind of authenticity that tourists are after when they visit a well-preserved but empty synagogue or rustic and rural church in Poland? For some it might be. Many of us carry a bias, often unconscious, that the older forms of life are somehow more worthy than ours. Somehow a modern person's real essence can be accessed through communion with the ancestors. Or somebody's ancestors, anyway. Tourists want to go places that feel authentic. Are there any among us, living in the contemporary world, who don't wonder if our own daily experiences, so mediated and abstract, actually constitute real life?

We are fascinated by authenticity. We want the privilege of being near the action, of experiencing what is true. Authenticity is about uniqueness, but that can be falsified too. What doesn't exist can be fabricated, imported. New Zealand has based an international tourism campaign on the *Lord of the Rings* movies, which happen to have been filmed there, and which tries to lure Tolkien fans to see the "real" Middle Earth.

On the other hand, we spend more and more of our time in spaces of oblivion—of obliviousness—surrounded by numbing, placeless homogeneity. In America, many cities still retain a lot of character and diversity. Being in Baltimore is nothing like being in New Orleans, which is nothing like being in Minneapolis or Los Angeles. But a few miles out of the urban core, if there is such a core, things start to look remarkably the same. Box stores, chain restaurants, clusters of name-brand hotels. Local color can be found, but it's well hidden and ultimately beside the point. These are environments built to reassure through repetition. They're built on the assumption that cheap real estate and plentiful gas are the building blocks of a culture all its own. Other countries have their versions of this, to greater or lesser degrees. Usually they look something like the American version, though rarely as big. A suburban everywhere. A disposable nowhere.

There is also a transnational style of oblivion: the austere vacuity of airports, worldwide hotel properties, convention centers, corporate headquarters, universities, and museums. Celebrity architects curate unfamiliar cities with clever, self-referential monuments to personal branding. High-end shopping has become nearly as predictable as McDonald's, even in places where most people live on less than two dollars a day. In his book *Cocaine Night*, about a professional travel writer, the novelist J. G. Ballard captures the scene of a posh resort that is an uncanny mix of exotic and banal, a place both alluring and anesthetic:

Already thinking of a travel article, I noted the features of this silent world: the memory-erasing white architecture; the enforced leisure that fossilized the nervous system; the almost Africanized aspect, but a North Africa invented by someone who had never visited the Maghreb; the apparent absence of any social structure; the timelessness of a world beyond boredom, with no past, no future and a diminishing present. Perhaps this was what a leisure-dominated future would resemble? Nothing could ever happen in this affectless realm, where entropic drift calmed the surfaces of a thousand swimming pools.

Arguably the consummate factory of fake experience is Disneyland. The French philosopher Jean Baudrillard called it the "palace of the imaginary." It's an environment where delight is manufactured. It is a simulation of the real world, but it aspires to something that the real world can't, by definition, produce—a Magic Kingdom where children can be happy at all times. Never mind that happiness is never constant, let alone guaranteed. For happiness to exist, unhappiness must be lurking somewhere in the background.

But not in Disneyland. Here everything is artificial: the food, the amusement, the emotions. You shake hands with Mickey, who isn't really a mouse. You scale a replica Matterhorn. You enter the inner parts of the human body. You see the pirates of the Caribbean, most of whom are made of wood. Everything is false in Disneyland, a kingdom of controlled happiness. And we're ready to pay as much as needed to give happiness to our children, if only for a weekend. In Disneyland, we're all naive children again.

Dubai, another global capital of fake experience, has built on the Las Vegas model of gathering the world's great sightseeing destinations into its desert oasis. It has replicated many of the ancient wonders of the world. It's the ultimate mark of anxiety for a place that is seen to lack authentic culture, or feels that way about itself. Inferiority is compensated for with audacity, sui generis self-invention. This quote from a 2004 story in *Wired Magazine*, back when Dubai was still booming before the global financial meltdown, says it all:

> As a Dubai tourist official once complained to an American journalist about Egypt: "They have the pyramids and they do nothing with them. Can you imagine what we'd do with the pyramids?"

Tourist travel is full of fake experience and falsified emotions: from joy to fear. A hotel chain in Bloemfontein, South Africa, called Emoya Hotel and Spa, invites tourists to stay a few days in a fake shantytown. The rooms are made of corrugated metal, cardboard, and other trash. Outdoor light depends on fires. The location is ideal: in the middle of nowhere. There are rooms for fifty-two guests. And you can't beat the rate: R850, the equivalent of €60 and US$82. Of course, certain ingredients common in shantytowns are absent here: crime, from domestic abuse to homicides; food scarcity; and especially overcrowding. Guests experience life rather comfortably. A video on the hotel chain's home page shows the rooms to be clean. There is running water. And wild animals roam around, giving tourists the sensation of living in a semirural environment. Never mind that most shantytowns spring up at the edge of developing cities and attract underskilled workers whose jobs dry up in the countryside. The closeness to the metropolis makes these surroundings "ugly" in the eyes of the more fortunate. The aesthetics are re-created in the Emoya Hotel and Spa experience, though it isn't the real thing.

Clearly the risk is too high to invite tourists to stay in real shantytowns. In the real slums, the company lacks a critical element: control. A real shantytown is dangerous. A fake one, on the other hand, leaves the variables in the host's hands. The thrills that come with the package—the exaggerated discomfort—are never left to chance.

Tourism has taken much of the arduousness out of travel, and certainly most of the danger. Albert Camus says in his *Notebooks*:

What gives value to travel is fear. It is the fact that, at a certain moment, when we are so far from our own country we are seized by a vague fear, and an instinctive desire to go back to the protection of old habits. This is the most obvious benefit of travel.

Even when the environments are authentic—at least compared to cruise ships or high-consumption desert oases like Dubai—we have actually arrived at a point where some people are willing to pay to have a little danger added back into the experience. Danger, even when contrived, is a difficult thing to manage.

In 2008, a forty-nine-year-old lawyer from Austria named Markus Groh traveled to the Bahamas to swim with sharks. He was a diving enthusiast, so this was by no means his first time underwater. But this trip, promoted by a company called Scuba Adventures, promised to up the ante. The company's motto was "No one gets you closer."

How? They took their divers out to sea, baited the sharks with chum (they were in Bahamian waters, sixty-five miles from Miami, because shark feeding was outlawed in Florida in 2001), and sent the intrepid tourists into the water without a protective cage.

Markus Groh was about fifty miles off the coast of Fort Lauderdale—swimming in the open water, presumably gliding through the bloody fish chunks that his handlers had dumped in to entice the sharks—when an unspecified sea dweller tore into his leg. The Coast Guard airlifted him to a nearby hospital, but his wounds were mortal and he was dead within a few hours. Groh was there to tempt fate by attempting the impossible: swimming in a sea filled with sharks. He wanted to prove himself; he wanted to experience a kind of freedom unlike anything he had tasted before.

Most people gave little thought to sharks before Steven Spielberg's 1975 thriller, *Jaws*. Since then, the fear and fascination inspired by sharks has become big business. Television programs like *Shark Week* are watched by millions. Some people develop phobias about swimming in the ocean, or at least avoid it; others do exactly the opposite—they become Markus Groh. Their attraction to sharks isn't scientific. They aren't interested in studying them. Instead, they study their own fear, seeking to tame it in irrational ways.

Groh created a theater in which he was the playwright, the director, and the actor. He played a couple more roles: the victim and . . . yes, the martyr. His death became public, which is what martyrs want: to be acknowledged, to perform on a stage for millions of people. The result is a death that repels as much as it attracts. It is insane, but our culture cherishes that type of insanity. We love immoderation, excess, extravagance.

Was he afraid? If you don't come back, at least you will have died an exciting death. And uniqueness is also meaningfulness. Die in your sleep and you're a bore. Die attempting the impossible and you are a hero. Our culture applauds those who push through the limits: they are like gods.

"Tourism is about travel that wants to imagine itself as innocent," writes the cultural historian Marita Sturken in her book *Tourists of History: Memory, Kitsch, and Consumerism from Oklahoma City to Ground Zero*. In New Orleans, after Hurricane Katrina, all kinds of outsiders descended on the city. Many came to help. Many came to document, make films, take pictures, write stories. In some parts of town, these were the only people you were likely to meet out on the street. The Lower Ninth Ward, a low-lying area almost completely submerged after the levees collapsed, became a focus of international attention. There were few buildings left intact and almost no residents. Large swaths of the neighborhood show almost no trace of their former life; today, the neighborhood has less than a quarter of its prestorm population. Many houses were just washed away. The fences that surround each plot are sometimes all that is left, as block after block has been overtaken by grass and weeds and swamp.

In the years following the storm, a small but visible cottage industry sprouted selling "Katrina tours," taking busloads of tourists to survey the wreckage. Tours that had previously covered the French Quarter and the Garden District now added a detour to see the world-famous Lower Ninth. Tourists don't get off the buses, so they aren't doing any good to the neighborhood economy. A lifelong resident told the *New York Times*, "I felt like an animal in a zoo. Videos of me are all over YouTube."

Disaster tourism, a facet of what has been more generally called "dark tourism," is another peculiar contemporary species. It has historical precedents, to be sure. Since the mid-nineteenth century, tourists have been visiting Civil War battlefields. Morgue tours enjoyed a brief popularity in Europe around the same time. Mark Twain writes about a visit to a Crimean War battlefield in 1867, while a passenger aboard the world's first long-distance cruise ship. He described his fellow tourists' strange impulse to take souvenirs from the grisly site:

> There was nothing else to do, and so everybody went to hunting relics. They have stocked the ship with them. They brought them from the Malakoff, from the Redan, Inkerman, Balaklava—everywhere. They have brought cannon balls, broken ramrods, fragments of shell—iron enough to freight a sloop. Some have even brought bones—brought them laboriously from great distances, and were grieved to hear the surgeon pronounce them only bones of mules and oxen.

Battlefields, death camps, natural disasters. Tourists visit Chernobyl (once furtively, now legally) and Fukushima, often bringing their own Geiger counters. Cambodia has been especially aggressive in marketing its genocide sites, the infamous killing fields, to tourists. In Andrei Tarkovsky's 1979 film *Stalker*, a tour guide takes two travelers into the Zone, a forbidden area that had been devastated by a meteorological disaster, an oasis with a terrible past.

In the 2011 tsunami in Japan, a forest of seventy thousand trees was washed away in Rikuzentakata, a beach town popular with tourists. Hundreds of years of growth were undone in a moment, except for one tree, which came to be called the "miracle pine." Then, a year or so later, the tree died. Its roots were exposed to saltwater. Local authorities spent a million and a half dollars on reviving and reinforcing it, in an area where debris was still being cleared to make room for new homes, with thousands still living in temporary shelter. The tree was sliced into segments, hollowed out, and reconstituted around a carbon spine. Now tourists come to see the tree that survived the tsunami—or something like it, anyway. The tree will be the centerpiece of a new memory park; the tree will be lit every night in commemoration.

The appeal of such experiences is complicated. In some cases, visitors come to connect with a personal or family experience. For decades after the Civil War, Grant's Tomb was among America's most-visited sites, and it remained so until the generation of Civil War veterans began to die off. Visitors to concentration camps are often similarly inspired, often children and grandchildren of camp survivors, or those who lost family in the Holocaust, or as part of a cultural education. Similar things could be said about the slave fortresses on Africa's Gold Coast or Robben Island in South Africa, where Nelson Mandela was imprisoned for twenty-seven years. President Barack Obama made highly publicized trips to both of these locations; the visits were presented as a mix of roots tourism and political theater.

In other cases, such sites have become just another stop on a typical itinerary, one more place to check off your list. In Berlin, the monuments and museums to World War II are a critical part of the city's branding and, importantly, an irreplaceable source of income. It's a big business with complicated ramifications for politics and culture.

The conjuncture of trauma and tourism is a sensitive, tangled place. It leads us to one of the most vexing questions of tourism, especially when we are coming to encounter the pain of others: Are we here to bear witness or to be voyeurs?

THERE IS ANOTHER side to the factory of fake experience: it is called folklore. Dean MacCannell, who has called the phenomenon "staged authenticity," describes it in the book *The Tourist: A New Theory of the Leisure Class*:

> For moderns, reality and authenticity are thought to be elsewhere: in other historical periods and other cultures, in purer, simpler lifestyles. In other words, the concern of moderns for "naturalness," their nostalgia and their search for authenticity are not merely casual and somewhat decadent, though harmless attachments to the souvenirs of destroyed cultures and dead epochs.

Countries invest in making themselves unique, distinct, with characteristics that make them memorable. Ever passed through a Swiss airport? You can't avoid the obscene varieties of chocolate, the red T-shirts, wool vests, army knives, and an assortment of tchotchkes designed to remind the traveler that this is what Switzerland is. How about stopping in Beijing? You'll be bombarded with silk fabric, straw umbrellas, and Chinese checkers. Each country announces to the world its DNA through a curated selection of stereotypes.

The most basic tool of the travel industry, ubiquitous for over a century, is the travel book. *France for $25 a Day. India in a Month. Macchu Picchu for Visitors.* These are the user manuals of tourist kitsch. So what are travel books useful for? To make the world accessible, to offer the keys to enter foreign doors. Travel books simplify kitsch, they make it palatable. How German is Germany? Open the Frommer's guide to find an answer. Generally, only certain information makes it to travel books: what the country wants to sell to foreigners, that is, the uniqueness of the place. It is branding. The South African novelist Nadine Gordimer, in an NPR segment called "Wise Words about Bettering a Troubled World," said:

> The country of the tourist pamphlet always is another country, an embarrassing abstraction of the desirable that, thank God, does not exist on this planet, where there are always ants and bad smells and empty Coca-Cola bottles to keep the grubby finger-print of reality upon the beautiful.

The difference between culture and brand is that culture enlarges while brand distills. Take Mexico as an example: its ascent is directly linked to a collective identity known as *mestizaje*. The mestizo is the by-product of the encounter between Spaniards and the indigenous population in the colonial period. Neither European nor pre-Columbian, this mixed breed is defined by its own cuisine, psychology, religious beliefs, pastimes—in short, a worldview.

The Mexican tourist industry arose in the late nineteenth century, as in so many parts of the world, as the country recognized its difference. It invited Europeans to visit sites that celebrated the heroism of Mexican cadets fighting the French army. It promoted natural resources connected with its ancestral religions. It turned its markets into bazaars. And it told tourists that the Mexican character was warm, hospitable, nonthreatening.

When Dwight Morrow was ambassador in Mexico in the late 1920s, that is exactly what he found. He collected souvenirs from open markets, which his friends insisted were "an authentic expression of Mexico's soul." Likewise, Graham Greene visited the country in the 1930s to chronicle the persecution of priests by the state (the result was his book *The Lawless Roads*, followed by his masterpiece, *The Power and the Glory*). In the end, he was uncomfortable, even angry. He was puzzled by the endless violence. Where he came from, violence was more controlled, less open.

"It's typical of Mexico," writes Greene, and "of the whole human race perhaps—violence in favor of an ideal and then the ideal lost but the violence just going on." To see violence up close, to experience it, to recognize that in Britain violence is subtle, less overt, pushed Greene to understand the contrast between the two civilizations, where he came from and where he had arrived. And, as his description goes on, he dwells in that violence, to the point of simplifying Mexico through it. In fact, it seems as if *The Lawless Roads* is a journey through Greene's own bewilderment: Is it possible that people in the twentieth century are still as barbaric? Barbarism, he concludes, is at the core of the human experience. He looks for it in his journey, almost thrilling when he encounters it. And when he doesn't, he asks people to replicate it. Greene writes:

> The man seeking scenery imagines strange woods and unheard-of mountains; the romantic believes that the women over the border will be more beautiful and complaisant than those at home; the unhappy man imagines at least a different hell; the suicidal traveller expects the death he never finds. The atmosphere of the border—it is like starting over again; there is something about it like a good confession: poised for a few happy moments between sin and sin. When people die on the border they call it "a happy death."

He wants violence because that is what he came to look for in Mexico. Take a trip to Mexico today and that is exactly what you're sold: pyramids, cockfights, mescal, danger! In other words, you'll feel as if you're witnessing Mexico at its most essential. You'll feel the fear Mexicans experience every day. Indeed, that fear is what you're paying for.

For Mexico to distinguish itself from the United States it needed, at the time of its independence, to stress its distinctiveness: its Aztec past, its tequilas, its mariachis with large sombreros, its spicy tacos. The added elements translated into a kitschy formula. (The Spanish equivalent for "kitsch" is *cursi*.)

It is important to define the word "kitsch," since it is essentially linked to the idea of fake experience. It comes from the German and is used in art to describe a cheap replica. *The Dictionary of Art*, in its 1998 edition, says the word means "pretentious trash, dialect, *kitschen*, to smear, *verkitschen*, to make cheaply, to cheapen." Thus, kitsch is more than a replica, it is the construction of a false sensibility. Walmart specializes in kitsch: for $25.99 you can buy a velvet vest with the Mona Lisa on the back; for $9.95 you can afford a box of Swiss chocolates made in Kansas; and you can buy a rifle just like the one used by Robert De Niro in the movie *The Deer Hunter*. Everything is just like something else: not the thing itself but a substitute, a fiction. The world of replicas is a place where authenticity is economized, made affordable to the masses. It gives the have-nots an honorary, temporary ticket to the world of the haves. What matters isn't the thing but its simulacrum. *The Dictionary of Art* continues: "A major function of kitsch in the present century is to reassure its consumers of their status and position, hence its association with the ever-nervous middle classes."

In Cuba, tourists flock to Santería ceremonies. The world of Santería in the Caribbean basin offers an allure to tourists, although it also projects danger—the type of fear Graham Greene talks about in *The Lawless Roads*. Westerners see the practice of voodoo as primitive. Yet the ability to manipulate the spirits of one's enemies is attractive to some people who live in a civilization purportedly shaped around reason.

For $500 a goat can be sacrificed before your eyes. That cost is twice what an average Cuban makes in a year. This means that the practice is a handsome source of income. An initiation rite might cost twice as much: $1,000. You can hear stories about the large flocks of Norwegians, Danish, and Swedish visitors coming down from a cruise ship to a Santería event; a major windfall for an island starved for foreign currency. The ceremony doesn't have to follow the rituals to the letter; it simply has to pretend. For the visitors are neophytes: they will take what is given to them as it if was the real thing. In 2007, a Reuters reporter described the experience in detail:

> After a fortune-telling session with Tarot cards or seashells, they offer to stay in touch by e-mail and urge foreigners to send over their friends. "Tourists come every day to see me. Mostly Spanish and Mexicans," says Laura, a voluptuous santera decked out in a tight lycra bodysuit and a mass of tinkling gold jewelry. "People come back to Cuba to see me or stay in touch by e-mail. I send advice and they send gifts. I even have 'ahijados' (godchildren) in France," she said, pausing to sell half a dozen $10 amulet bracelets to a Mexican tourist clutching a wish list from his friends back home.

This speaks to the way tourism can debase and devalue a cultural experience. What is offered to foreigners is a summary—a condensed version of the actual practice. But for many, that version seems to be enough.

"Sentimentality," according to Carl Jung in an essay on James Joyce's *Ulysses*, "is the superstructure erected on brutality." This is how kitsch works in a political context. Political kitsch is the division of the world into helpless victims and godlike heroes. Is the absence of basic regard for other humans based on shared humanity (in this way, it is a noxious kind of anti-cosmopolitanism); political kitsch is cheap emotion masquerading as morality. Tourism is a branch of nationalism. And nationalism is built on kitsch. This type of kitsch is visible on the National Mall in Washington, DC. A visit to the nation's capital is an opportunity to travel through an assortment of contrived spaces—and fake experiences—designed to awaken in us feelings of patriotism, of devotion to the United States. Just as Mexico sells its unique cultural story, the National Mall is a pageant of American exceptionalism. Various branches of the Smithsonian offer visitors a chance to witness the extraordinary scientific and technological advances made in the United States. There is a museum for American Indians. Look, the place declaims, our nation was built on suffering and we are all the better for it. The United States is built on difference. And museums play upon that difference to accentuate the nation's motto: *e pluribus unum*—in plurality we become a unit. They underscore American values, distinguishing them from those of other countries of the world.

Museums, as tourist destinations, turn memory into a theater whereby you can become a protagonist in history: the Founding Fathers shaping the Constitution, Abraham Lincoln minutes before his assassination, the first astronaut setting foot on the moon. On the way out of the museum, you are invited to stop at the gift shop and buy a hat like the one George Washington wore while crossing the Delaware River, or a mask like those used in Shakespeare's last play, *The Tempest*. Souvenirs are the material companions to kitsch. They allow you to take the experience home with you. You will always have a memento.

As you enter the U.S. Holocaust Memorial Museum, you are given a fake passport that is also an itinerary. It belonged to an individual who went through horrific experiences during the Nazi era. With that document, you become that person. The objective is to personalize the odyssey, to make it concrete: as the catastrophe is taking place, you become a victim. You feel what a Warsaw ghetto dweller felt. You are brought to Auschwitz. You see the crematoria, the gas chamber. You endure. Then you are greeted by American GIs. You wander through the ruined streets of Europe looking for your relatives. You are lonely, depressed, and hungry. Eventually you immigrate to British-mandated Palestine. Or to Ellis Island. You settle in Chicago, or St. Paul, or Los Angeles. And you begin a new life. Is that really you? Yes, you are the other and the other becomes you. The museum has enabled you to be a witness. "Living history" has become a pedagogic cliché. The kind of immersive personalized experiences that characterize many museums today are not catalysts for empathy, only narcissism.

Political kitsch has also gone transnational. An interesting, and distinctly contemporary, variety is the emerging business of birthright tourism. These are programs, with destinations as varied as Ireland and China, that bring youth from various diaspora communities to encounter their ancestral homelands. Here is where the tourism industry converges with a major dynamic in global geopolitics, which Benedict Anderson called "long-distance nationalism." Anderson commented on the trend to Audra Lim, writing in *Dissent* magazine:

> "It's not just identity and it's not just tourism," he said. "The homelands also know that it's important to have effective lobbyists in America. Pressure is put on the people there to defend the motherland and whatever the motherland has going for it."

Every year, tens of thousands of teenagers travel to Israel on a program known as Taglit-Birthright Israel ("taglit" is the Hebrew word for discovery). Similar programs exist with names like Birthright Armenia and Ethiocorps and In Search of Roots (for Chinese Americans).

In 2011, the Israeli government approved over $100 million in funding with the goal of bringing half of the world's Jewish twenty- and thirtysomethings to Israel by 2013. The premise behind it is that every Jew in the diaspora has a place in Israel, the Jewish homeland, and that inviting youngsters will enable them to grasp its magic. The trips are fully subsidized for the participants. There is an ambiguity to Birthright's objectives that is extremely sensitive, because it arises from a deep ambivalence among American Jews about their relationship to Israel. In the group's own words, "Birthright Israel's goal is to enable young people to experience Israel as part of a larger effort to strengthen Jewish identity, Jewish communities and solidarity with Israel." If that seems vague, it is intentionally so. No American Jewish organization could build the kind of broad support that Birthright enjoys if its goal was explicitly to recruit young people to Israel. Forty years ago this may have been palatable, but not today. In truth, the crisis in the Jewish community that prompted Birthright had little to do with Zionism, but rather intermarriage and assimilation.

The group also must be circumspect about the politics of the Israeli-Palestinian conflict. At the very least, organizers must be muted in their advocacy, even if the organization's name sends a loud and clear message about a territorial dispute with citizenship at its heart. In the absence of tangible goals, we get abstractions like "identity" and "solidarity."

What happens is a kind of Holy Land pageant, where Israel becomes the stage for a high-production-value performance, a pitch for Jewishness to young Jews. On the website Buzzfeed—a barometer of the zeitgeist in 2014—a "listicle" called "42 Signs You Went on Birthright" offers some thoughtful takeaways, such as:

10. Seven miles, 15K steps, and 2000 daily calories burned later, the first night out reminded you how beautiful Jewish girls can look when they have a few minutes to get ready. . . .

11. You also realized every Jewish guy's wardrobe consists entirely of J. Crew, Banana Republic, and Lacoste. . . .

17. You heard incredible stories from people around the world who share an amaaaaaaaazing passion for Israel and whose personalities can only be described with one word . . . Trippy.

Across the border from Israel, a perverse new tourist attraction practices another variety of political kitsch. The Tourist Landmark of the Resistance, which is also known as the Museum for Resistance Tourism, was designed by Hezbollah in Mleeta, a village in southern Lebanon. It opened in May 2010, "marking the tenth anniversary of the Israeli withdrawal from southern Lebanon." They have spent millions on this theme park and have attracted 300,000 visitors from Lebanon, neighboring Arab states, and all over the world.

Guides welcome visitors to "the land of resistance, purity and jihad." The primary purpose of the museum, if it is even necessary to say, is to tell the party's own story and communicate its worldview. Kids show up at the park in miniature paramilitary costumes. They carry plastic AK-47s. They play inside decommissioned tanks, crawl along barbed wire and into replica bunkers. They can aim weapons at Israeli-uniformed mannequins. If the battlefield at Gettysburg was turned into a miniature golf course, this is what it would look like.

The program, in style and presentation, is not so different than what you'd find at the Smithsonian or the Ronald Reagan Presidential Library. You begin in a theater, where you are shown a film telling the Hezbollah story. There are historical displays, artifacts, and infographics. A *Vanity Fair* article sets the scene:

> We walked along another path and saw mannequins of Hezbollah guerilla fighters in various combat poses. There was a replica of a field hospital, a machine gun children could play with, and a monument to the "Martyrdom Seekers," as suicide bombers are called. ("They make the ultimate sacrifice," our guide said; he did not comment about the victims.) The restrooms are done up in a camouflage motif.

Nothing is out of bounds for tourism, and there is nothing so degraded that it cannot be glorified. The world is messy, ambiguous, and indecent, but kitsch distorts our picture of the world in ways that flatter our own feelings. It is not a world of human beings, in all their complexity, only heroes and villains, perpetrators and victims. The world of kitsch is a simpler world with very bad guys, very good guys, and causes so righteous that no blood or dirt can taint them.

Milan Kundera, in his novel *The Unbearable Lightness of Being*, defined this kind of kitsch perfectly: "the absolute denial of shit."

EPILOGUE

Home Is Where

The traveler sees what he sees,
the tourist sees what he has come to see.

G. K. CHESTERTON, *THE TEMPLE OF SILENCE AND OTHER STORIES* (1929)

Julio Cortázar, the Brussels-born Argentine author of *Hopscotch*—
a novel, structured as a mandala, which you can enter from multiple doors—has a little-known gem of a story that might explain
what moved him to leave home for Paris, where he lived the rest
of his life. The story is called "The Band." The story is set in 1947
and dedicated to the French surrealist René Crevel. Lucio Medina,
a film aficionado, tells Cortázar, the author and narrator, the hu-
morous plot. Years before he leaves Argentina, forever giving up
his career and possessions, he goes to the Grand Opera Theater
to see a film by Anatole Litvak announced in the local paper. He
changes his schedule to fit in an early performance. He arrives,
buys a ticket, and enters the theater. Nobody has bothered to tell
him that the show has been canceled. Instead of the movie, he gets
a band of ridiculous teenagers: Banda de Alpargatas, a group of
Perón-sympathizing cheerleaders.

Medina can't believe his eyes and ears and for a while he thinks
he has landed in the wrong theater. He sits quietly in the audience,

thinking he might be watching an opening act, but the band keeps on playing one terrible song after another. Bewildered, oversaturated, and furious, he finally stands up and leaves, feeling like a victim of the official culture. But days later, he realizes the event had a larger meaning: the band he hears is a symbol of the small-minded nationalism closing in on him. This epiphany mirrors the author's own. Cortázar's parents took him to Buenos Aires when he was little. He stayed there until his thirties, when he no longer could tolerate the Peronistas, a regime that redefined Argentine life as populist tyranny.

A single incident, insignificant at first sight, suddenly changes our life forever. It tells us that we are on a journey. Unbeknownst to us, we were traveling on a road that took a sharp, unexpected turn, and voilà—we are no longer the same. We are no longer at home. These are the amplifying moments of seeing beyond our own subjectivity. Sometimes they are the moments that start us on our travels, which first alert us to the potential of a larger world, and they are the kind of moments that nurture us in our travels and keep us coming back.

The protagonist in Cortázar's little parable is not simply struck by wanderlust. What he experiences is a total reorientation in time and space. His world had lost its center; he was set into motion because, suddenly, home was not where it used to be. If there is anything distinctive about life in the modern world, it is this: the notion that home can also travel.

Home and away are not fixed categories. Our sense of home will change many times over the course of our lives, just as our address will change and maybe even our homeland. Our homes leave deep marks in both time and space: in earliest childhood, home is about proximity to our parents. Our mothers' arms are where our most primal sensations of belonging reside—does it even matter in what country, or on what street, or in what apartment we were first rocked to sleep? In those formative days, our home also delimits the boundaries in which we can safely explore the unfamiliar world. Meaningful travel begins at home. As adults, we associate home with familiarity, but as children, home is our first laboratory and uncharted terrain.

One is only intermittently a tourist, at most. Being a traveler is something we can aspire to at all times. Learning to be better travelers might also help us become better citizens, more vigorous in our encounter with the world. Eudora Welty, in *One Writer's Beginnings*, says, "Through travel I first became aware of the outside world; it was through travel that I found my own introspective way into becoming a part of it."

In our endlessly networked world, we have many tools at our disposal to simulate the sensations of discovering new places and interacting with different people. Some of these encounters are necessarily shallow or frivolous, though others can be substantive and profound. Given the resources at our disposal, why should a person still make the effort to travel in the real and nonvirtual sense?

The mobile phones in our pockets can do extraordinary things for us. Sometimes it feels like they can deliver the world itself. Being plugged in validates our existence. What defines us is the name, number, and expiration date on our credit card, our Facebook page, our Twitter account; it can feel sometimes like we are the sum of our various accounts, that we are the data we mindlessly send up into the cloud to be parsed and harvested and sold back to us by others.

More and more, the tourist feels like an apt symbol of contemporary life. There is a kind of revulsion at the passive acceptance we associate with tourists (at least in caricature), with the cheapness and emptiness of prepackaged experience that mirrors the anxiety we feel in our commodity-rich but attention-starved societies. We probably all feel at times like we are being herded through daily life, watching out from behind glass, craving real feelings and connections but settling for something less demanding.

Of course, tourists are not merely metaphors, not just projections of other people's insecurity or disdain. Tourists and travelers are not different species. Most people have probably been—or felt like—both at some point in their lives. Any self-styled traveler has had that experience of awkwardness and mild self-reproach when he finds himself at that site that feels just a little too obvious and touristic. Am I just a tourist? Am I just one of *them*?

Really, there is no *them*. All kinds of experiences can coexist within even the most overdetermined itinerary; there is no trip so homogeneous that every group member experiences everything identically. Tourism doesn't happen outside of history, and this holds for both the individuals and the sites. There are gaps that get filled in with past experience, prejudice, and personality. So it's important to distinguish the individual desires of tourists from the industry that promises to realize them.

The business of tourism is to make us reliable voyeurs. While the voyeur might know how to look, she doesn't see much. What is the difference between looking and seeing? Looking means gazing at something and, by doing so, recognizing its presence. Seeing means much more: it implies understanding, maybe even acceptance. The voyeur looks whereas the observer sees. The voyeur is removed, protected from the object of fantasy while the observer is involved, even committed to it.

Deep inside, as consumers and voyeurs, we are dissatisfied. We want adventure. We crave experience. We don't want to see ourselves as cogs or statistics. That hunger makes us want to move, to encounter new things, to travel to different places. So what basis do we have for a new approach, a new ethic of travel? Like most good and necessary things, most of it will not be new.

"The ultimate ethical test for tourists," Dean MacCannell argues in *The Ethics of Sightseeing*, "is whether they can realize the productive potential of their travel desires or whether they can allow themselves to be mere ciphers of arrangements made for them." This means that we are all responsible for the content and the consequences of our experiences. Because the goal is to realize our own desires, we can't chart the course for anyone other than ourselves. Yours will not look like your neighbor's. It matters who you are, where you're going, and what you hope to find (or lose).

We have an ethical requirement to be informed visitors. We have an ethical requirement to be considerate and curious guests.

The final film by the great Indian filmmaker Sagit Ray is called *The Stranger*, and it is a dazzling rumination on travel and change. The plot is simple enough. A man returns to his home city after decades abroad. He has almost no family left except for one niece, and he invites himself to stay in her family's home. The homecoming and reunion are not meant to be permanent; he's just passing through, on his way to somewhere else he hasn't been yet. The relatives aren't sure why he's returned—they think it might be to claim an inheritance—and greet him with both curiosity and suspicion. He's been gone so long but no one remembers his face. It's as if his travels and experiences have made him into an unrecognizable creature, no longer part of the family and life he left behind. His niece asks him tenderly, uncomprehending: "Why did you leave home? Everyone loved you."

"There is a wonderful German word: 'Wanderlust,'" he answers. "It means the irrepressible urge to travel." He describes a revelation, as a young art student, upon seeing the image of the prehistoric cave paintings of bison in the cave of Altamira. It ignited in him a fascination with both civilization and savagery. It awoke an urge to explore.

But they are not just suspicious of his motives; they don't understand the life he has led. A life of travel and adventure—and solitude—seems to upset their own sense of belonging. He fascinates and scares them at the same time. The conversations become interrogation: Who is this man? What does he want? Is he still a part of their world?

Above all, he is being asked to justify his life of travel. One of his interrogators, a family friend who is a lawyer, exclaims, "If you are someone or no one is exactly what we are trying to determine!" From their perspective, the traveler might have no identity at all.

But travel is his identity; curiosity is his flag. In a deft twist, we learn at the end that he has come to write a travel book: an Indian among Indians. He is one of them, but no less an outsider. Home is another scene to explore.

WE ARE IN DESPERATE NEED of a new approach to travel. But it won't be easy to achieve, so entrenched are our patterns of behavior. What is needed is a thorough reconsideration of why we search for ourselves and how we engage in that search.

So how should we reclaim travel? We can start by recognizing all the ways in which the world today is more available to us than ever, and take responsibility for our own experience and our impacts. We should strive for a productive relationship with discomfort. Foreignness is uncomfortable. Uncertainty is uncomfortable. Even voluntary, temporary displacement brings uncertainty. But uncertainty is conducive to self-knowledge. Travel enlarges us because it is an opportunity to explore other possibilities for our lives: how things might be different had we been born into another circumstance; how our life might have been different had we made different choices; and, above all, what life could look like for us in the future, if we had the courage to make certain leaps into the unknown.

Reclaiming travel doesn't necessarily require avoiding tourist sights, for those can be sites of rich experience, too. The key is to be alert even while one is traveling the beaten track. This type of travel isn't confined to a particular demographic. It is for everyone. All of us journey depending on where we are in life. To reclaim travel is to recover the capacity to wonder, regardless of age, gender, ethnicity, and economic status.

Gustave Flaubert, in his diary of the travels he made to Egypt, wrote, "Travel makes one modest. You see what a tiny place you occupy in the world." This, after all, is a movement of return: a return to the myths that have served as traction—and as public dreams—for countless civilizations; a desire to know the multiplicities that make up the universe without reducing them to digestible and unthreatening categories; a rejection of the glib and facile and an embrace of ambiguity, which in the end is the way the world presents itself to us: as never-ending contradiction.

In short, a return to ourselves. The ultimate paradox of travel is that it can be return, escape, and search at the same time. We travel to free ourselves from the environments and expectations that feel too limiting, too constrictive. But those who are deeply compelled to travel are also looking to find a place in the world that feels more like home, where we can be both more completely ourselves and also less alone.

We might never find such a place. It's a promise that stays with us and keeps us moving.

ACKNOWLEDGMENTS

Wholehearted gratitude to Mark de Silva for bringing us to the attention of the opinion page of the *New York Times*, where our piece "Reclaiming Travel" originally appeared as an editorial, and to Peter Catapano and Simon Critchley for their savvy editing of it. Gracias to Miriam Angress, our editor at Duke University Press, for visualizing the piece as a full-length book, for reading it with unending enthusiasm in its various stages, and for readying it for the editing process. The comments she requested from an assortment of anonymous readers allowed us to sharpen our argument. Their insight and professionalism are admirable. We feel in debt. Thanks also to our production editor, Liz Smith, for shepherding the volume through production, and to Karen Fisher for an eagle eye as copyeditor. In and of itself, the making of *Reclaiming Travel* has been a memorable journey.

INDEX